HOLDING HANDS WITH GOD

Rivers of Living Waters

JIMMIE L. CHIAPPELLI

WESTBOW
PRESS
A DIVISION OF THOMAS NELSON

WestBow Press books may be ordered through booksellers or by contacting:

WestBow Press
A Division of Thomas Nelson
1663 Liberty Drive
Bloomington, IN 47403
www.westbowpress.com
1-(866) 928-1240

Because of the dynamic nature of the Internet, any web addresses or links contained in this book may have changed since publication and may no longer be valid. The views expressed in this work are solely those of the author and do not necessarily reflect the views of the publisher, and the publisher hereby disclaims any responsibility for them.

Any people depicted in stock imagery provided by Thinkstock are models, and such images are being used for illustrative purposes only.

Certain stock imagery © Thinkstock.

ISBN: 978-1-4497-7343-4 (e)
ISBN: 978-1-4497-7344-1 (sc)
ISBN: 978-1-4497-7345-8 (hc)

Library of Congress Control Number: 2012920670

Printed in the United States of America

WestBow Press rev. date: 11/12/2012

Preface

Hello! My name is Jim Chiappelli, called by God to bring unity to the body of Christ, and to help establish His kingdom in His Church.(Remember you are His church) My wife Karen and I, have come to realize, that we need unity in the body of Christ. As co-laborers together we will continue to strive to bring about the unity that's needed to bring God's people to maturity.(Or do we need maturity, to realize we need unity, I think both.) This is a time when God desires maturity in His people. Furthermore, we realize that this is going to happen with or without our input. However, we feel blessed that God chose us to contribute to this cause. Our prayer is that we can prepare the way for others so that they will come to a more mature relationship with Jesus Christ. And by Holding Hands with God, and one another, we can be co-laborers with Christ for His purpose. -AMEN-

DEDICATION

I thank the Lord Jesus Christ for never giving up on me, and for always being faithful to me. Even when I wasn't always faithful to Him. And to all the people He sent to accomplish His goals. This includes all the people, who gave unselfishly of themselves, to be builders of God's kingdom. From the people who picked us up as children to take us to Sunday school, to the people who nurtured us along. I know I can't mention all of their names, I'm sure I don't even know all their names . Even the people who worked behind the scenes, and I would like to let them know that their works are a reflection of their faith.(See James 2:17-18 faith by itself, if it does not have works, is dead. But someone will say, you have faith , and I have works. Show me your faith without your works, and I will show you my faith by my works.) and here is a partial list of some of those people the Freeman's, the Shover's, the Dell's, the Koppelburger's, the Koreiba's, the Chiappelli's, the Bills, and the Covarrubias family and on and on. -Thank you and may God bless you.-

Chapter 1

THE BEGINNING

Hello. My name is Jim, and this is my first book. I hope you will enjoy it. This is not an instructional book. After all, there are thousands of instructional books out there, and besides, I'm not sure you should take instructions from me, even though I'm full of them.

This is a story or testimony about faith, hope, love, and obedience, not in any particular order, as you will see. I would like to start at the beginning. Not at the very beginning of time, but I mean my beginning.

I was born in 1948 and named Jimmie Lee Chiappelli. I was the second of ten children: eight girls and two boys. Yes, I am a baby boomer. I am eighteen months younger than my sister, Yolonda, and six girls later, we had another boy, Tony. The set was finished with one more girl.

I'm not sure bowling or other recreational activities had been invented at that time. I did learn later though, that the number of children my parents had wasn't accidental. My dad I learned, had decided very early on to have twelve children, and I don't think my mother had too much to say about it. Things were different back then. Women didn't have too much to say about their futures.

My first memories as a child took place at 314 Prospect Street in Pontiac, Michigan. At that time, there were four of us: Yolonda, me, Diana, and Cindy.

I didn't have much contact with my dad because he wasn't around much. I'm not sure he knew what his role was as a father. The reason I say this is because we were always hungry and didn't have any clothes to speak of. We had cracks in our walls and dirt floors.

I vividly remember my sister Yolonda and me collecting snow from those cracks in the walls. There were times when my sister and I had only one outfit each. As we got older, we often washed our outfits by hand and hoped they were dry by morning.

When we lived on Prospect Street in Pontiac, we often slept on a hide-a-bed with my mother in the living room to keep warm. We were extremely happy and didn't realize we were poor. I think we had a special closeness because of these adversities.

I don't think television had been invented yet at least not for us. However, we did have a radio to listen to, and it was great. Weekends were wonderful. My dad would come home load us in the car, and take us to our grandparents' house, on Florence Street a few miles away. That's when the fun would really begin. We all congregated—the adults together and the children together. If you could walk and you were not wearing a diaper, it was pretty certain you were going outside.

The older ones watched out for the younger ones. It wasn't a perfect system, but it worked most of the time. There were a few injuries but nothing serious. If someone got hurt, going inside wasn't usually an option. That usually meant playtime with your cousins was over.

There was a bunch of us, and at that time, we ruled the neighborhood, but not in a bad way. We knew that if our behavior was out of order, there would be consequences. Back then, that meant a whoopin. Now, if you're younger, you probably don't know what a whoopin' is. I had three sons, and they definitely knew what it meant, but it's a different story for my grandchildren.

I can remember one particular instance when one of my grandsons was misbehaving. Jokingly, I asked if he wanted a whoopin. He looked at me, somewhat puzzled but very seriously, and asked, "What is a whoopin?

"It's something I used to give your dad when he was your age."

He said, "Could I have one?"

Jokingly I said, "Well, maybe later." I don't really believe in whoopin's anymore. And besides, my grandchildren never do anything wrong.

Getting back to the family: it was a large family. Keep in mind, my grandmother and grandfather had ten children, and some of them had large families. As you can imagine, that home on Florence Street was always packed, especially on weekends and in the summer.

We were all very close and weren't afraid to show it. We became very protective of one another.

Okay! Now that you know something about me and where I came from, I will continue where I left off.

When talking about the books I mean all those instructional books it's hard to know where to start. Have you been to the bookstore recently? I know when I first became a Christian or let's say when I rededicated my life I was around thirty-two. I

3

started reading every book I could get my hands on, especially books that were written by other Christians. After a while I became so confused I didn't know in which direction I needed to go. This was a difficult time in my life because of the conflict inside of me.

Prior to my conversion, I was an atheist and had given a great deal of thought to that topic and to the topic of evolution. I was extremely confident in what I believed or didn't believe. I had developed every argument to prove God doesn't exist. And anyway, how about evolution! Didn't our schools teach us about evolution and how we evolved from a substandard species?

This, in my opinion, totally eliminates the work of our Creator. If you really think about it, you will realize evolution is completely ridiculous. Sit down and think about it sometime: Did half a bee pollinate a half of a flower? Or when did egg-laying animals decide to put shells on? As you can see, it's no wonder our children have become so confused. I could go on and on and on for hours, so I'll drop it right here. I will address this topic more in my next book.

All right, let's get back to the story. As I mentioned previously, I had become a very confident individual, but around age thirty-one, my life began to unravel. It seemed as though everything I did was starting to fail. My business, my marriage, it seemed like everything was failing at the same time. And every decision I made seemed to be wrong.

I could go through a long description of these failures, but they're all pretty common. I don't want you to think I had no spiritual or religious background or training. That wouldn't be true. Early in my life, at around seven and a half, I had my first experience with God. That was the first time I had ever heard His voice.

It was at a little church on Green Street in Pontiac, Michigan. I remember that first experience vividly and how I asked Jesus into my heart. I told some of the other children, but they thought I was a fruitcake. Oh, maybe they were right. If you don't think God speaks to us today, you too might think I'm a fruitcake. Just kidding!

I can remember Yolonda, Diana, Cindy, and me attending that little church. I don't remember my parents ever attending, but I do remember my spiritual growth. In retrospect, I greatly appreciate the people who picked us up regularly in spite of any of their other obligations.

I believe all of us can bring these people to mind if we think back. I know that I can. I can actually remember their names and how hard they worked to build God's kingdom. These are the ones who went before us to prepare the way just like John the Baptist prepared the way for Jesus Christ. These people didn't sit around and watch to see if they could see God's kingdom coming. They knew by faith that it was coming. If it weren't for people like them, God's kingdom wouldn't be in the glorious condition that it's in today.

My wife, Karen, and I can see God's kingdom being established in His temple and in His people more and more every day. I would like to put a special emphasis on the latter part of this Scripture. Keep in mind that God is building this temple. **(Luke17:20–21) states. The kingdom of God does not come with observation; nor will they say, See here! Or See there! For indeed, the kingdom of God is within you."**

We believe that God's people, His church, His temple are finally coming to the realization of who they are in Him and who He is in us. Although we should also remember that we are not all in the same spiritual location. After all, He does say:

> **In My father's house are many mansions; if it were not so, I would have told you. I go to prepare a place for you. "And if I go and prepare a place for you, I will come again and receive you to Myself; that where I am, there you may be also. "And where I go you know, and the way you know." (John 14:2–4)**

You know He's not talking about heaven. He is talking about our abiding place in Him, His abiding place in us, or a place of indwelling of the Holy Spirit.

> **If anyone loves Me, he will keep My word, and My father will love him, and We will come to him and make Our home with him. (John 14:23)**

The first time I read this was in the King James Version of the Bible, which says, if a man love Me, he will keep my words: and My Father will love him, and We will come unto him, and make Our abode with him. There are not going to be different classes of people in heaven or different houses to live in. He is talking about a spiritual location or a place of maturity that we can go to now.

Keep in mind that He says in **(1 Corinthians 13:12) "For now we see in a mirror, dimly, but then face to face. Now I know in part, but then I shall know just as I also am known."** We see here again that He is talking about our maturity. Again in **(Galatians 4:1-2) He says, "Now I say that the heir, as long as he is a child, does not differ at**

all from a slave, though he is master of all, but is under guardians and stewards until the time appointed by the father."

This Scripture sort of reminds me of my three sons when they were growing up. They were under my care and guidance, and I so wanted to protect them from anything and everything so that no harm would come to them. However, I soon realized maybe not soon enough that I had to let them go and grow and make their own mistakes. I had to have the confidence that God can finish the work that He starts, and that God takes the mistakes of His children and uses them to build the character He wants in each and every one of us.

This is what God does for us. He lets us go so we can grow. But keep in mind, God will never leave you or forsake you, just as we will never leave or forsake our children even though we have wanted to a few times. In fact, I think we have, but they keep finding us. (Just kidding!)

We know that when we first become Christians, our maturity level isn't there yet, but every day we will see Christ in ourselves. As we do, we will see Christ in others. I can remember very early in my walk with Christ, I had a great deal of doubt, even though I had experienced a tremendous vision, as I'll tell you about later. I was in a place where I felt I had to see something tangible. I mean, how can you worship a God you can't see? But I continued to seek God and went to church at every opportunity.

However, on one particular Sunday during worship and praise, I said to God, Lord, I don't know if I can continue if I can't see you."

He said, "Jimmie, open your eyes."

I opened my eyes and said, "Lord, where are you?

He said, "If you want to find Me, you will find Me in My people."

I could actually see God's presence descending upon His people. This gave me a whole new love for God's people once I realized that God dwells in His people, (His temple) we are His temple. In (Haggai 2:9) God says "The glory of this latter temple shall be greater than the former,' says the Lord of hosts. And in this place I will give peace, says the Lord of hosts." Now remember, here again He's talking about us. We are His temple! **(Hebrews 11:10) say's "For he waited for the city which has foundations, whose builder and maker is God."** Now let's look at **(Jeremiah 18:1-6)** "Here again God talks about being our Maker:

> **The word that came to Jeremiah from the Lord, saying: "Arise and go down to the potter's house, and there, I will cause you to hear My words." Then I went down to the potter's house, and there he was, making something at the wheel. And the vessel he made of clay was marred in the hand of the potter; so he made it again into another vessel, as it seemed good to the potter to make. Then the word of the Lord came to me saying: "O house of Israel, can I not do with you as this potter?" says the Lord. "Look, as the clay is in the potter's hand, so are you in My hand, O house of Israel!**

He is not just the builder and the Maker. Don't you see we are that marred vessel, and He can remake us into His image! If we go unto the mountain of the Lord, He will teach us to dwell in that temple or house in peace. **(Isaiah 2:3) says, "And many people shall come and say, come and let us go up to the mountain of the Lord, to the house of the**

God of Jacob; He will teach us his ways, and we shall walk in his paths; For out of Zion shall go forth the law, and the word of the Lord from Jerusalem."

Karen and I, after traveling all forty-eight lower states, and after talking to many other Christians, feel that there's some confusion, about where God's temple is. Some people actually think that God's temple is being built somewhere over in Israel, and that mountain of the Lord referenced in (Isaiah 2:3) is located somewhere over there. I'm not saying that the building of God's temple in Israel doesn't hold some significance. I don't really know. All I'm saying is we should be looking at His spiritual temple.

We need to think about this for a minute. Can you imagine if all God's people traveled to Israel and tried to climb that mountain at the same time? It would be pure pandemonium. So remember, all God's people are in different places. First comes the natural or our physical location in His Kingdom, and then comes our spiritual location or our spiritual abode or maturity in Him. We should always try to remember that it's not our geographical location God is talking about; it's our spiritual location or maturity.

And besides, you know He's not talking about our geographical birthplace. God is talking about our spiritual birth. (John 3:3) says, **"Most assuredly, I say to you, unless one is born again, he cannot see the kingdom of God."** There are no exceptions to this that I can find in God's Word.

(Galatians 3: 28) says, There is neither Jew nor Greek, there is neither slave nor free, there is neither male nor female; for you are all one in Christ Jesus. "You see, it's not your nationality or what tribe you come from. If you are born again, you are an heir with Christ.

Well I think I've said enough about that. Keep in mind, this is my first book, and sometimes my spiritual maturity isn't exactly what I would like for it to be, if you know what I mean so go easy on me. And besides, I have a help mate, you know, my wife, who reminds me of this occasionally, sometimes more than I like.

One night Karen and I were talking and laughing about our spiritual immaturity and how patient God is to dwell with us regardless of those faults or our inability to mature at times. We came up with this little saying: "Lord, it seems to us that every time we think we have reached our destination, we realize our train hasn't even left the station." Karen and I are extremely thankful that God doesn't ever give up on us and will never give up on you. Remember, God will never leave you or forsake you. We live by His grace.

Back row, left to right my dad holding my brother Tony, my mom holding my sister, Clara, Yolonda, me front Diana, Cindy holding Nancy's hand, Narda also holding Nancy's hand then the twins Leaha and Lisa.

Left to Right Marc, Jim, Karen, Me and Tim

My beautiful wife Karen and I

Grandchildren, from left to right Noah, Emma, Chloe, Darian, Marcus, Serena, and Joshua.

Chapter 2

GOD'S GRACE

My mother taught me how to pray at a very early age you know, that "now I lay me down to sleep" prayer. I think we were all taught that same prayer when we were young. I was always thankful for that prayer, and I used it every night. Even though my mother didn't attend church, I always knew she was a special person. As I learned later, she had made a commitment to Christ early in her life.

My dad was a different story. Although I've been told he made an early commitment to Christ, he didn't show any fruits. You know the ones I'm talking about. Besides, he was never home, and I never understood how a person could be at work twenty-four hours a day and not provide for food, clothing, and other essentials needed to raise a family. I'm not sure that he knew what his role as a father was, although I will say he started to take interest in us eventually. When I was around thirteen, he even started attending church, and I could see a change in his behavior. But at that point in my life, I'd pretty much done everything on my own, and I was not really interested in what he had to say.

When I was around age thirteen, he decided that we were going to move to Santa Monica, California, and it was a really difficult move for all of us because of our family. We didn't

Jimmie L. Chiappelli

want to leave our family but looking at this in retrospect, I know that my dad was looking for a new start. It wasn't as though he didn't try for a new start in Michigan, but because of his past, he soon learned that no one would accept him as a new person in Christ. He knew that the only way he could be the man he was supposed to be was to move to a place where no one knew about his past.

That's exactly what he did, and that's when he started to bloom. He started to be the man God wanted him to be. Unfortunately, the older children didn't trust his ability to provide. After all, we judged him by the past as well. I think we were tired of being hungry and without clothes and guidance. We started to look elsewhere, and in so doing, we started doing things we should not have been doing. Besides, I knew very well that I could stand on my own two feet, so I went to work first as a paperboy, then at a market, and then as a painter in Long Beach, California. I went to work with my brother-in-law, and he taught me the trade.

As you can see, because I started to earn my own money, I became even more independent. I bought my own food, I bought my own clothing, and I made my own decisions. Sometimes those decisions weren't tolerated by my dad, so the war was on. It's extremely difficult to start taking orders from someone when you've made all your decisions on your own.

It's very possible that if I would have known how he felt about me or the rest of us, I might have been able to have listened to him. I'm not sure. It wasn't until the very end of his life that I started to realize how much he did care. Even now looking at this in retrospect, being a father myself, I can see that he had changed, but because I had become so independent and had been making my own decisions, I couldn't accept his authority. He was trying to force his authority on me by physical punishment. This punishment did not border on child abuse: it was way across the border I think he thought he was doing this for my good.

When I was seventeen, my dad was forty-one. He was on his way to work at his second job. After all, he had ten children, and you certainly can't provide for ten children with one job. As I said before, when we were growing up very early on, he was not a good provider. However, even though he and I were at war, I now realize looking back that he was working diligently to provide for the younger children.

I usually worked with him at night but had learned how to make myself scarce when it was time to go to work. After all, I was paying my own way now. I sometimes paid the house payment and often paid the car payment, and I knew in which direction I wanted to go. I knew I could make it on my own, but like I said before I could see a change in him. We had started to communicate on a very limited basis. We'd had a tremendous falling out, and I told him point blank, "You will never beat me again." After all, I thought I was pretty tough and wasn't afraid of anyone.

He had great plans for me, but they were not my plans. Besides, I had already developed a mind of my own. After that falling out when I was fifteen years old, he never beat me again. I don't know what would've happened if he had. I'm sure one of us probably would have been in jail or the hospital, or maybe both, but I knew the beatings were over, regardless of what had to happen, and I know that he knew that as well. When I look at it now, I realize that I had become just like him extremely headstrong wanting my own way at all times.

As I mentioned previously, after my seventeenth birthday, which was April 12, it was actually five days later, he had left to go to his second job. Within a few minutes, he returned home. He explained that he had felt this tremendous pop in the back of his head. Then he stated he needed to lie down for a while. Not wanting to leave the job undone, he asked my brother-in-law, Ron, and I if we would go and do the job. We said yes and left very shortly to do the job. I knew the job had to be done or else. And I knew that we needed the money.

Ronnie and I were extremely efficient together, and we made short work of the job and returned home within an hour. Upon our return, I asked my mother how my dad felt, and she said that he had gone to sleep but was still complaining about pain in his head. I decided to go in and talk to him, and as I entered the bedroom, I could see that he had urinated on himself and knew this wasn't good. Then I looked over at his desk and seen that he had been reading his Bible, and thought, this is not good either, not that it's not good to read your Bible. However, because of the tremendous pain he was in, I didn't think he would be reading his Bible. It was then I decided it was time to call an ambulance.

Yes, it was my decision! Very early on in life, I learned to make my own decisions. They weren't always the right decisions, but they served me well. I've just always been the type of person who didn't panic in emergency situations. At that time we did not have a telephone so my girlfriend Karen, and I went to the corner to call an ambulance. At that time, there was no such thing as 911, so we had to call the operator. She put us in touch with an emergency unit, and we explained to them briefly what had transpired. They told us that the ambulance was on the way, so we returned home.

My mother was waiting for us at the door. She asked us if we had called. We told her we had. and we proceeded to wait. We waited approximately two hours and decided we had better go call again, so we made the same call. They answered the phone again, and we told her that the ambulance had not arrived. She said, "I didn't know it was that important, and by the way, do you have insurance?" We told her he did. She said. "That's a different story. The ambulance will be there within minutes."

We returned home and relayed that information to the rest of the family. When the ambulance arrived, the attendants came into our home, asked us a few questions, and started slapping him in the face. They said, "How long has he been drinking?"

I said, "my dad doesn't drink."

"Has he been using drugs?" they asked.

I said, "No he hasn't!" I explained again what had happened, and at that time, my dad woke up and said, "What's going on here?" This was while they were putting him on the stretcher. He exclaimed, very sharply, "You don't have to carry me. I can walk."

At that point in time, he closed his eyes and went back to sleep, or so we thought. Now I know he had gone back into a coma. The ambulance took him to the hospital, and we followed in the car. After several hours, the doctor came out to the waiting room to tell us the news. The news was not very favorable. They said your dad has suffered a massive brain aneurysm, and we have given him blood clotting agents to stop the bleeding. Although, it was such a massive bleed, if they couldn't stop the bleeding, it would reach spots in his brain that control the functions of other organs, and would bring about his death. However, they couldn't do surgery unless they could stop the bleeding.

At that point in time in my life, I had pretty much lost whatever communications I had with God. But I was not going to allow that to stop me from finding God, so I went to a private location to seek God. And guess what? After a very short period of time, He started to speak to me, and He was very clear. He said He could not give me what I was asking for, and no matter how long I continued to ask, He continued to give me the same answer.

As I left the chapel and started walking back toward the emergency room, as I looked down the hall, I could see my brother-in-law, the doctor, and our family pastor walking toward me. As they got closer, I actually tried to avoid having contact with them, but I wasn't able to do so. They informed me that my dad had passed away just a few minutes ago. It was absolutely devastating! After all, like I said before, my father and I had really just started to communicate, and I wasn't ready to lose him at that time. I don't think we're ready to lose our parents at any time, but after the tumultuous, violent past that we had together, I was anxious to continue to establish a relationship with him.

Looking back, I can now see the miracle that God was doing in his life. He was actually asking me questions, not only asking them but waiting for my response. Before it was, "You have nothing to say. I don't care what you have to say. You have to do what I say." I know that these changes don't come easily. Let me tell you why as I said before, I had become just like him and didn't care much about what others thought or said. He had started to accept me and some of my decisions. In accepting me, he was accepting the things I thought were important.

One of those things in particular was the girl of my dreams. Now when I tell you this story, you're probably going to think it's corny, but being the hopeless romantic that I am, I just have to tell the story. It was a short time before my fourteenth birthday when I started to think about girls. I didn't know what all their uses were, but I knew they were better looking than boys. As I told you earlier, I had lots of sisters and wasn't afraid to talk to girls, but I knew my mind was starting to go in that direction.

A short time before my fourteenth birthday, two of my friends came over and asked me to go to downtown Santa Monica to just hang out or look around at the scenery. Okay, the girls. There was an overabundance of them in downtown Santa Monica. We had done this many times before, but this was different. We walked into a store called Newberry's, and on the other side of the store, I saw the most beautiful girl I've ever seen in my life. It was like this store was totally empty except for her. I was totally captivated.

She was wearing a blue sweater and black slacks or capri's or whatever you want to call them, and white tennis shoes. As soon as I saw her, I knew she was going to be my wife. I know this sounds ridiculous, but it was just something I knew. I told my two friends, Jerry and Henry, "That's going to be my wife." They laughed hilariously for a few minutes, and then we moved on to another store. After all, we did go to look at the girls, but I couldn't get my mind off the one in Newberry's. Besides, my mind was already convinced I had met the girl, I had dreamt about. I thought to myself, *I will probably never see her again.*

I know I told you before that my relationship with God wasn't very good, but this was something that I prayed about. I asked God to make it possible for me to see her again. About one month later, we moved to the house on Third Street. We needed a larger house because we had outgrown the two-bedroom cottage where we were living, although I think we outgrew that house before we moved into it.

I was attending a school in Santa Monica called Lincoln Junior High and wanted to finish the year there. I got in some trouble for fighting, like usual. When they found out we had moved, I was asked to leave. I would be attending John Adam's.

But before I started school, a friend came by that night and told me about a girl he had met. Then he asked if I would ask her to go to the show with him. He knew I wasn't afraid to talk to girls.

I agreed, and come to find out, lo and behold, this was the girl of my dreams. This girl lived right around the corner from our new house. Our backyards actually met, although I didn't know that at the time, and there was a small fence separating our yards. I'm not sure, but I think I wore that fence out. Not wasting any time, we walked around the corner. Now remember, I didn't know that this was the girl of my dreams. I went up to the house and knocked on the door, and guess who came to the door? Yes, it was the girl from Newberry's.

My heart jumped for joy. I didn't know if I was dreaming or what, but I did know my friend was going to be out of luck. I said, "Hello, my name is Jim. I just moved in around the corner and have seen you around, and I'd like to know if you would like to go to the show."

She replied, "Yes I would, but I will have to ask my parents first."

In those days we used to walk to the show. It was like a date but not really. So the next day I went up to her house to see if it was going to be okay, and her dad came to the door and started asking me questions. It was like an interrogation. He asked what my beliefs were, what my plans were, and almost everything you could imagine. I must've answered his questions right, although I believe I must've made some of them up because I didn't know what my plans were, except I knew that she was my plan. After all, I was only fourteen, and didn't have any plans, except taking his daughter to the show.

After we talked for a long time, he agreed that I could take his daughter to the show with a few exceptions. I had to keep a close eye on her, which was not a problem. I knew I was going to keep a close eye on her and that I would stay close to her, which wasn't a problem either. He also stated I had to protect her and not allow anything to happen to her. I agreed to all those terms. If he had asked me to climb Mount Everest, I am sure I would have agreed.

I would like to say I don't believe in love at first sight. There are too many emotional factors that enter into that equation of love. But I did know that for some reason, Karen and I had somehow bonded. She and I have talked about that meeting in Newberry's extensively since we have gotten older, and she tells me, that she had very similar thoughts. This tells me this was not an accidental meeting. God always has a plan, and that plan will always come into existence. But always be cautious and don't try to force His plan.

From that point forward, Karen and I were almost inseparable, and she started integrating herself into our family. It seemed as though she was readily accepted by everyone, with the exception of my dad. He somehow thought that Karen would ruin my ability to succeed, or ruin my plans.

What he didn't realize was I didn't have any plans in life before I met her. After all, I was from a poor family of ten children and had pretty much given up on myself. But after meeting Karen, seeing her academic excellence, and knowing I wanted to be a part of her life, it gave me the initiative to strive to be a better person. And with her help, my grades started to improve, and so did my attitude.

Now that Karen and I have been called to the ministry, we get opportunities for people to talk to us about their marriages. It's always the same story. For some reason, men always tell us the story about how that their wives and children have ruined their lives and plans for success. The women feel the same way.

We need to all realize God made us for one another and that we are one another's plan. We need to quit blaming each other for our shortcomings and realize that because of our relationship that God has given us for one another or with one another, we can do all things in Christ. He will be made perfect in our weaknesses.

Read **(Genesis 3:12-13) Then the man said, "The woman whom you gave to be with me, she gave me of the tree, and I ate.** You'll notice Adam said, "The woman you gave me." Yes! God gave women to us as our helpers that we might stand together as one. **"And the Lord God said to the woman, what is this you have done? And the woman said, the serpent deceived me and I did eat."** Okay! Where was Adam? Wasn't he supposed to be with Eve so she could have someone to talk to?

I don't know about you, but if you're married, are in a relationship, or have the opportunity to talk to women, I think you'll find that they do like to talk a little more than men do. However, as I've gotten older, I think Karen would argue that point. But probably the first twenty-five years of our marriage, I think she did most of the talking.

I can remember at a particular point in our lives, when Karen asked me why I never talked to her. I very calmly explained that I didn't want to interrupt her. I know I paid for that comment for a long time. However, I knew I would never say it again. I think Adam was off doing his own thing, and Eve became lonely and had no one to talk to. That's sort of like it is today, don't you think! Men are off doing their own thing football, baseball, hockey, hunting, fishing, the ministry, etc. yes even the ministry.

I always tell my sons, when they ask me about these things, when their wives want to talk to them that in fact they should even initiate these open lines of communication for sharing. I always tell them, "You can listen to your wife and communicate with her or she will find someone who will." And we also need to realize that if our love for one another is what it's supposed to be, it won't be a hardship. It will be something we look forward to regularly very regularly, and it will cause both of you to reach for a higher calling. Keep in mind love is the answer, but forgiveness is essential for maintaining that love. And remember that two people walking together in unity as one can accomplish almost anything.

Chapter 3

THE KINGDOM

Well, I guess before I go any further in this book, I should tell you what my beliefs are just in case they offend you. You may want to read something else. Anyway, here's what I believe. Besides, I need to get back to how I came up with the name of this book.

Okay here it goes: in the beginning, God created the heavens and the earth. I don't know how long ago He created them, but I know He did. There has been a great deal of controversy about how old the earth is. Some people say it's billions of years old, some say its six thousand years old, and some pick numbers in between. But as for me, I know something that they don't know, and that is that they really don't know. And besides, in my opinion there will never be enough scientific evidence that will prove how old the earth is or who created it.

We know, just because we know **(2 Corinthians 5:7) says, "For we walk by faith, not by sight."** After all, we believe by faith, not by scientific evidence. And besides, doesn't God's Word say that we walk in faith? In **(John 20: 29) Jesus said, "Thomas because you have seen Me, you have believed. Blessed are those who have not seen and yet have believed." Now let's look at (2 Corinthians 4:18)**

While we do not look at the things which are seen, but at the things which are not seen. For the things which are seen are temporary, but the things which are not seen are eternal.

We need to believe in the things that are unseen because if we need evidence of God's existence, then we probably should reevaluate this thing we call faith and keep in mind the reason we know that He lives is because He lives in us. There is evidence of that life in us by the fruits we produce. That's why I know God created the earth, and I know He created it for us. **(Genesis 1:26) says, "Then God said, let's make man in our image, according to our likeness; let them have dominion over the fish of the sea, over the birds of the air, and over the cattle, over all the earth and every creeping thing that creeps on the earth."**

Dominion, as defined in (Webster's New World Dictionary Fourth Edition Michael Agnes Editor in Chief copyright 2003 by Wiley Publishing Inc. Cleveland Ohio Page 195) to rule or have the power to rule. He put us in this beautiful garden to care for it and watch over it with His guidance. But because He created us with our own free will, He knew we would want to do it on our own. It reminds me of our own children.

I know my first son, Jim, as he started getting older I think it started around age two he started wanting to do everything on his own. His shirts went on backward. His pants went on backward. His shoes went on the wrong feet. He wanted to tie his own shoes. He wanted to help me cook. He wanted to help me work.

I can remember a certain incident that happened one time. He was two years old, it was Friday, and we were going out to eat. He was standing in the back seat of the car. I looked back at him to see what kind of job he had done. Okay, I liked looking at him. Actually, I still do. Then I noticed his boots were on the wrong feet.

I said, "Son, your boots are on the wrong feet."

He looked down at his feet for a second and then looked up and said, "Dad! These are the only feet I have."

That's how God made us, we always want to do things on our own. And even as adults, we often continue this type of behavior, and just as we look at our children with that love, this is the way God looks at us. But He did have a plan that He knew would reconcile us to him. This was his plan from the very beginning. And oh, by the way, we are His plan His only plan.

For a long period of time, He allowed us to do our own thing. Then He sent lots of people to tell us how to conduct our lives and to show us who He is you know, the prophets! But most of the time we didn't listen. So at the appointed time, He sent His Son to earth in the person of Jesus Christ, born of the Virgin Mary, conceived by the Holy Spirit. I am sure He thought *I can't believe that this is who they think I am. Now it's time to go show them.*

He came to His own, but they wouldn't receive Him because He was not what they wanted or what they perceived God to be. I think we all make decisions about who God is based on our own mindset. I know I have. I often judge Him by myself. I believe we do the same thing today. Often times He reveals Himself to us and we don't recognize Him because it's not who we think He is. **(John1:11-13)** says:

He came to His own, and His own did not receive Him. But as many as received Him, to

them He gave the right to become the sons of God, even to those who believe in His name. Who were born, not of blood, nor the will of the flesh, nor of the will of man, but of God.

He actually became sin, died on the cross, and even made sin a spectacle to all. **(Colossians 2:14-15) says:**

Having wiped out the handwriting of requirements that was against us, which was contrary to us. And He has taken it out of the way, having nailed it to the cross. Having disarmed principalities and powers, He made a public spectacle of them, triumphing over them in it.

He arose, came back to life, and became our high priest. He ascended into heaven and sent His Holy Spirit to guide us. He went to prepare a place in Himself so He could receive us to Himself. I believe He chooses us first. He asks us to marry Him and to be His bride. Then we must choose of our own free will if this is who we want to marry.

This is pretty much what I believe. I know there are a lot of doctrinal beliefs or truths that need to go in there, such as you must be born again. You have to receive the Holy Spirit for guidance and a whole bunch of other stuff. But if I put all of my beliefs down, I wouldn't have room to write anything else in this book, so there you go. That's pretty much what I believe. It's simple, yes. Like I said before, there's a whole bunch more stuff you need to know, and as I learn these things, I will try to share them with you. Maybe in another book ha, ha.

Now for the name of this book, and how I got the name. As I mentioned earlier, at around age thirty two, my life had started to unravel. Even though I had acquired a great deal of success, I wasn't happy and started to question my atheistic beliefs. I didn't know at the time, but I was about to have a life changing experience. And it seemed as though every place I turned, there was someone trying to tell me about God. But I was not going for it.

I thought to myself, *if there is a God: He will have to reveal Himself to me.* Even though I knew the other road or world system had taken me to the wrong destination, it was still difficult for me to give this control of my life to someone I didn't know. Looking back, I now realize God had strategically placed all of these people in the exact location He wanted them. After a time, I decided to see what they were talking about. I was somewhat apprehensive at first, but as things continued to deteriorate, I had nowhere to turn.

One night I don't know how long it took, I think it was a few months. Karen and I went to bed, and I couldn't sleep. I knew I didn't want to live the way I was, so I slipped out of the bed, got on my knees, and said, "If there's any such thing as God, please reveal Yourself to me." Immediately a tremendous light came in to the room. I was instantly terrified and tried to cover my eyes, but the light penetrated my entire body. When He touched me, my fears were completely gone. I felt only peace, joy, love, and rest. It was the first rest, I had felt in years.

This light was so bright, I couldn't see what He looked like. It was almost as though His clothing was light, but I knew immediately who it was, and I knew I wanted Him. Then He spoke to me. He didn't say a lot, but what He said was memorable. He said, "You pray for My presence, and you're not ready for My presence. So prepare yourself for My presence."

That was all He said that night. That doesn't sound like much, but it was the first time in a long time that I had heard His voice. I wasn't exactly sure what He meant by this, but I knew I wanted more of His presence. So I started to read everything I could get my hands on you know the books. There were hundreds of them telling you what to do and what not to do: how to stay married, how to treat your wife, how to treat your sister, how to treat your brother, how to pray, how to act, how to worship, how you get to heaven.

There were so many rules and laws that, to be quite honest with you, I could not keep track of them all. Now I know how the original children of Israel felt with all these laws. And almost every one of these books, with a few exceptions, had a different idea of what you are supposed to do. After a while, I felt like that song that says, "You got me going in circles." I was spending so much time learning the to do's and the not to do's that I didn't have much time for anything else.

Unfortunately, I couldn't find Him in those books. Fortunately, there was a book available I hadn't tried yet. It was the Bible. My sister Yolonda had given me a Bible. I think it was for my birthday. It was the King James Version, which I started to read diligently, and as I continued to read, I also continued to pray and seek God. Every night after my wife went to sleep; I would sneak down to the living room and seek Him. And every night as I sought Him, I would raise my hands. I actually felt His hand in mine, and so came the name of this book, *Holding Hands with God*. And for some thirty years, I have continued to hold hands with God. If you ever see me at church and see my hands held high, you'll know that I am holding hands with God.

Now back to the visitation. Wow! What a visitation. I was so excited I couldn't wait to tell everyone. I mean, after all, I didn't realize that God didn't talk or appear to people today.

But as I learned that's what most people think. However, every night He would come to me and talk to me. The first one I tried to tell about this encounter was my wife. I couldn't wait for her to wake up so I could tell her. I think she thought that I had lost my mind. Although I am not really sure what she thought, she didn't want to hear about it.

We got ready and went on to work, and I proceeded to tell my customers. *Oh!* I forgot to tell you I was a barber. I started to tell all my customers what had happened. I can remember the first one, and what he said. He said, "So you're telling me, Jim, that you've seen the light."

I said, "I guess I am."

He said, "It's about time! Now maybe you can see to give me a good haircut."

Then I proceeded to tell every customer, and as I did, my customers started to go elsewhere, with the exception of Christians. Even some of them didn't want to hear about it, but most were glad to hear about my new found faith. However, the rest of the clientele or customers weren't very understanding. I continued to tell them whether they wanted to hear it or not, not realizing they didn't want to hear. As I tried to continue to witness to these pagan unbelievers (just kidding), my clientele continued to dwindle.

As I realized later, they were in the same place I had been for such a long time, and the only training I had received was watching other Christians forcing or trying to force God on others. After running off most of my clientele, my business was really going downhill fast. I thought, God is going to restore this business, but it was not happening.

Now I don't want you to think that I didn't have some wonderful Christian customers, because that wouldn't be true.

Their loyalty and patronage through those very difficult times brought some stability. Some of the older ones who had been successful in business tried to give me advice, but I wouldn't listen to what they had to say. I mean, after all, who knew more than me?

But as God continued His visitations and the scales started to fall from my eyes, I started to see myself as I really was, and because of God's love and patience, I knew that God was changing me. **(Second Thessalonians 2:3-4) says,**

> **Let no one deceive you by any means, for that day will not come unless the falling away comes first, and the man of sin is revealed. The son of perdition, who opposes and exalts himself above all that is called God or that is worshiped, so that he sets as a God in the temple of God, showing himself that he is God.**

Some people seem to think that this is talking about a great falling away of Christians from God's kingdom, but I know this is talking about us and how, as the scales fall from our eyes, we start to see and hear. We come to the realization that we have exalted ourselves above God and we actually think we know more than God does. I was one of those people with scales on my eyes. I couldn't see my sin until the falling away.

There were a great many bright spots. One of them was my cousin Loren, who was just starting his ministry. He was my first cousin on my mother's side and was completely different than other Christians I had met. Instead of talking, he would listen before he responded. And more importantly, I continued my nightly holding hands with God, reading His Word, and taking His instructions. God told me over and over, you know the Christians you had contact with in your younger years. You know the ones who wanted to tell you everything you were doing wrong. You know the ones you wanted to kill at times. They were appointed by Me at an appointed time to build My kingdom. But I want you to know this is a new time. I am going to do a new thing in this earth, and I want to use you, at an appointed time, to help bring about the necessary changes in my people, but if you become indoctrinated, I won't be able to use you, so try to avoid contact with certain individuals I will point out to you. I will place godly people in your life for training and to teach you who I really am."

The following morning, as I remember, my first customer was my cousin Loren. I knew from that day forward that he would be my pastor and mentor. I could actually see Christ in him. He had just recently opened a small church called Mount Zion in Clarkston, Michigan, and he invited me to attend. It was different than any church I had ever attended, and I felt somewhat comfortable there. Because there wasn't very many people in attendance yet. When he spoke, he wasn't a screamer, and that was good for me. He got his point across or God's point across, without screaming or yelling. The things he was saying were almost exactly what God was speaking to me.

I knew that I was in the right place. And besides, *I thought, If I'm crazy, it must run in the family.* Wow! I think that was prophetic. Yes, I said prophetic, not pathetic. Then, I decided to take the understanding God class for adults. My son Jim, who had already been attending church at Mount Zion, courtesy of my sister Yolonda, would be attending as well. What a great way to start learning how to understand who God is. I would like to say this class led me into areas of revelation I could never have imagined. I believe it should be mandatory for everyone. I know my growth would not have come so effectively without this class, and I thank God for that class.

Chapter 4

DEATH AND RESURRECTION

I would like to clear a few things up. I don't want you to think that I'm being critical of other Christians or of our Christian forefathers, and my hope is that I haven't said anything to offend you. That was not my intention. I am extremely thankful for early Christians who have gone before us and prepared the way for us. My hope is that we Christians today can prepare the way for future Christians or God's people. Furthermore, I hope that God's chosen people will continue to seek His wisdom through worship and prayer to build His kingdom. Because this is the way God chose to build His kingdom, line upon line, precept upon precept. Okay! Now I can continue.

As I continued to seek God I took all the classes I could take, because I knew I had a calling on my life. You have to remember, we all have a calling, and that calling is to reveal Christ to the world, through our actions, our deeds, our speech, and our love for one another. I knew my calling was to be in the ministry full time, and I was extremely excited. (I just didn't know it would take some thirty years of preparation.)

Unfortunately, my wife didn't share in the excitement. I had received a prophetic word for my wife, which was that she would be rivers of living water and that she would be a pillar for me in the ministry and a whole bunch more stuff. I thought to myself, *I'll continue to study, seek God, and do my own thing and she'll have to follow and do what I say. I mean after all, I am the boss, ha, ha.*

As I continued to walk in this new direction, she was not following. I know now she was tired of following me and had already decided to look for a new leader. The reason I know this is because, years later, we discussed this topic extensively, and Karen is always extremely truthful. She has shared all of her thoughts she had during that time. This was a very volatile time in our lives.

When I realized she was looking for a new captain or leader, I did everything I could do to change her mind. I worked diligently toward that goal, and things just continued to worsen. I would clean the house, do the dishes, and buy her flowers. I would listen to everything she had to say, give her all kinds of compliments, and do every possible thing I could think of (Remember I said previously I had read every possible book you could read on marriage.)

The problem was these were not coming from my heart, and I think all women have some sort of discernment about these things. After a long period of time it seemed like years; I guess it was! I soon realized I had become the best wife my wife could ever have, and I did not like that role. There was very little participation on her behalf, especially when it pertained to anything concerning the church.

Sundays were extremely hectic, and she totally refused to participate. I had to get up, get the three boys ready, feed them breakfast, and make it to church on time. I was always late, and I would sometimes wonder, *what's the use? This is not working.* But as I continued trying to walk in the direction I knew God wanted me to walk, she continued to walk in the opposite direction. I didn't know what to do next. I didn't believe in divorce. Other Christians were insistent that divorce was a sin and that after the divorce I would be responsible for her sin every time she had relations with another. That would hold true for me as well, and I could never be forgiven, no matter what. However, I knew in my heart that I had to make this decision.

Don't get me wrong I am not an advocate for divorce. However, I do believe that if an unbelieving spouse walks away, that a brother or sister is no longer under bondage (contract) to that person. **(First Corinthians 7:15) says, "But if the unbeliever departs, let him depart; a brother or a sister is not under bondage in such cases. But God has called us to peace."**

This is a really touchy subject to Christians. Somehow we Christians have adopted a belief system that we use to try to control others. But you know and I know that telling somebody it's a sin to prevent him or her from doing something has never worked and never will, except on a temporary basis. However, at that point of time in my life, I believed that they were right. Being very frustrated and not knowing what to do, I asked my wife if she would agree to go to counseling. She said, "No! I don't need to go to counseling; you do." So I went.

I was learning a great deal about myself, about marriage, and about relationships, but the situation at home was not changing. One day as I was seeking God, I believe God spoke to me, out of Job (not my favorite book). I'm not going to repeat all of it, just the verses that were important to this decision I had to make:

> **Now prepare yourself like a man; I will question you, and you will answer Me; Would you indeed annul My judgment? Would you condemn Me that you may be justified? Then**

adorn yourself with majesty and splendor, And array yourself with glory and beauty. Then I will also confess to you. That your own right hand can save you. (Job 40:7-8,10,14)

God said, "You need to stand up like a man and take the responsibility of making this decision, or you can continue on and let her make this decision. Don't you see? Your wife has walked away from this marriage."

I said, "Lord! I don't think I can do that."

He said, "If you do what I tell you to do, I will give you someone who you will love twice as much and someone who loves you twice as much."

I said, "Lord, that's not possible!"

That was all He said at that time. However, not wanting to make a mistake, and because of my emotional state of mind. I wanted to make sure I was listening properly; I went to see my pastor. He said, "Jimmie, I know you hear from God, and I believe if God told you to file for divorce, that's exactly what you should do."

I don't think that's what I wanted to hear, but never the less I knew I had to be obedient. So I served Karen with divorce papers the following day. She says she was completely devastated and didn't think I was capable of making that type of decision. But she didn't appear to me to be that upset at that time. She tells me now that she knew immediately she had pushed me too far.

She got her attorney, I had my attorney, and the war was on. I moved out of the house at first, for two weeks anyway, but I still continued to attend church and take my children. But after two weeks, I was at church, and God spoke to me again! He said, "Go home." I knew it was Him. I was learning through this situation to hear His voice. I packed up and headed home.

Now, there were a lot of things that were going on during this time, but it would take three or four books to tell you everything that happened. Let's just say God was there at every twist and turn. I knew, even though I had returned home, that my decision for divorce was final, and I had no intention of turning back. But I also knew I couldn't afford to pay the house payment, the car payments, and rent at another location. I decided, because of those circumstances, and because of what God had spoken to me, that it was time for me to go home. That's what I did.

The first week was horrifying. I'm not sure, but I think Karen was trying to get me to choke her. But as time went on and I refused to get angry, I could see a change in her. It was very subtle at first, but every day it became more and more apparent. However, I had already made up my mind, and besides, I didn't think I could trust these changes. As days went by and I continued to seek God, He started to open my eyes and plow up that fallow ground or soften my heart so I could receive seed, and then we started to communicate with one another in a whole new dimension.

Remember, if our marriage had been on the right road, it would not have ended up in that destination (divorce). After all, we did have three children in common, and we really needed to communicate. I now realize when I was doing those things before my heart just wasn't in it. You know the housewife thing. I was only doing those things to try to make her love me. But after filing for divorce and not having any thought of reconciliation, I was able to listen to what she had to say, and as her feelings started changing toward me, my heart was starting to soften.

Although we battled for six months in the courts, or our attorneys did, we were becoming one again! She started coming home from work I mean straight home. She would make dinner, clean house, and everything she used to do. Don't get me wrong. As I said previously, our marriage was never restored to its original place. If our marriage was what it should have been, it would not have wound up in divorce. Unfortunately, our divorce was so costly that we wound up losing everything, except for the most important thing (each other). As things got worse financially, we drew closer and closer. I soon realized she was not the same person, and neither was I.

As I sought God about this, He said, "Because of your obedience, I gave you someone who loves you twice as much as the other one, and one who you love twice as much, just like I said I would." So one day away from the finalization of our divorce, I called my attorney and stopped the divorce. Karen was overwhelmed with joy. After we lost our house, our business, our savings, and our pride, we moved into an apartment, but we were happy again. Our marriage continued to blossom. I could never have dreamed of having a marriage so wonderful. By the way, now we were making decisions together, and I had a great desire to share this decision making process with my wife.

After living in Michigan for thirty-one years, and all of our children were raised and out of school, we decided we were going to make a move to Arizona, for the weather and for a new start. As we were making plans to move, my wife's sister called from California, asking if we could care for their mother. Because of our commitment to family, we didn't hesitate to make that decision. After all, Karen loved her mother, and so did I.

They said it would only be six weeks, and we could continue our move to Arizona. Two years later, we were still there, working diligently for a departure to Arizona. We worked from dawn to the wee hours in the morning for months. Finally the time had come. We packed up our van, our U-Haul and our two dogs and left for Arizona. That was in May of 1998.

Both of us went to work and started earning a great deal of money. Although my wife had changed dramatically, she wasn't ready for God, but didn't resent my participation. She would occasionally attend church physically but didn't seem to want more. So for six years, I continued to seek God. I would like to say, even though Karen wasn't willing to attend church, she had become a wonderful and caring wife. God had restored ten times what we had lost in possessions with a new house, two new vehicles, and plenty of money in the bank. Our savings was ten times what it was in Michigan.

Things were going so fantastic that we couldn't believe it. But on October 27, 2004, our lives were changed forever. My son's ex, Angela, had stopped by for a visit and brought the grandchildren. She and my wife were visiting on the porch. I had made my wife a sandwich and went out to the porch to tell her that her sandwich was ready and I had to go pick up our son from class. Angela replied that if we would babysit, she would pick Tim up. It was a good fit for us. We loved being with our grandchildren.

When she left, our grandchildren went to their playroom, and I sat down with my wife to visit while she was eating. After eating dinner, she went to the bedroom to change out of her work clothes. The phone rang, and it was my sister Yolonda. She was in the hospital, she explained, and was going to have a stent inserted in her heart in the morning.

Knowing that my wife would want to be in on this conversation, I followed her to the bedroom, but the door was locked. I heard a loud noise, and I called out to her, but there was no answer. I called out again, and there was no answer. As I put my ear to the door I could hear a noise that sounded like, I'll say, gurgling. I told my sister, "Sis, there's something wrong with Karen. I have to go."

I tossed the phone to the floor and broke down the door. I could see Karen lying face first on the tile floor, and I immediately went to her aid. I turned her over, and she wasn't breathing, I listened for a heartbeat, and there was no heartbeat. I immediately picked her up, carried her to the bedroom, and laid her on the floor. It was like a dream. I stepped back and said, "God help me."

I don't know how long I waited to regain my composure, but I soon realized, if I didn't take immediate action, it might be too late, so I started CPR. I don't know how long I worked, but it was quite some time, and finally, she started to breathe; not a lot, but a little. I listened for a heartbeat, and there was a heartbeat. It was very faint, but it was there. I immediately reached for the phone and called 911. The dispatch lady asked for my address, which I gave, and commenced to give me directions for CPR. I told her I had already given her CPR.

Almost immediately there was a knock at the door. It was the EMS. You see, we were only a few hundred yards away from the fire station. As EMS attendants and emergency workers flooded into our home, the whole neighborhood started coming to life, and I could see crowds gathering outside, along with it seemed ten or fifteen emergency vehicles and fire trucks. As I talked to the paramedics, I explained what had happened and that I thought that she had suffered an aneurysm.

They said, "How would you know that?" I explained that my dad died from one and that her symptoms were very similar. I think that got their attention, because I heard two of them talking. One of them said, "We should take her to Barrow," and the other one said, "We don't go to Barrow," and the other exclaimed "Tonight we do!" as they proceeded to work on her tirelessly.

As I learned later, they lost her twice but continued to work. They explained again, after putting her on life support, that she was in a deep coma, and her condition was very serious. My grandchildren were oblivious to what was going on, and quite honestly, I had forgotten they were there. I immediately called a friend, Jim Aurelio, who lived about one half hour away, and as neighbors started gathering around the house, there were actually, a couple of the neighbors inside the house. I didn't know who they were. They didn't even speak English. I think they were speaking Korean all I knew was I had never seen them before, but my mind was starting to work again.

I recognized a young couple. I called them over and asked if they would watch our two grandchildren. I already knew they were trustworthy, and they agreed immediately. Besides, I didn't want our grandchildren to see their grandmother in this condition. As they were wheeling my wife out of the house, my friend Jim was just arriving. I asked if I could ride in the ambulance. They said no, and after my friend talked with them, he offered to drive me. As I talked with him a few months later, he told me that they told him not to hurry because she was not going to survive.

When I arrived at the hospital, I went straight to the emergency room. They asked me my name and ushered me to a private room, I think. I'm not really sure. I don't think I would've known if anybody was there or not. Then they gave me the devastating news: My wife of thirty nine years had suffered a major brain aneurysm, so massive that there was very little chance for survival. However we needed to wait for Dr. Spetzler's evaluation.

They asked for my consent to insert a shunt to drain the blood because of the massive bleeding. I quickly signed a consent form and then dropped to my knees and started to pray. My son Tim had arrived at the hospital, along with Angela his ex, and they were praying right along with me. The hospital staff continued to give me updates on her condition. None of which were good. In fact, they said I needed to notify any family members of her condition, so I went outside and started calling. I called my oldest son Jim first and then my second oldest Marc. They lived in Michigan. They were absolutely devastated. I think I talked to their wives first. I can't remember, but I did explain that if they wanted to see their mother alive, they should come immediately because that's what I was told by the hospital emergency staff.

Chapter 5

WRESTLING WITH GOD

I made all the necessary calls to our children and her family. Now this is where my memory is just a little sketchy. I don't remember the order in which I made my calls. After all, my wife of thirty-nine years, my companion, my best friend, the love of my life was lost. As I recall, my next call was to my pastor, my cousin Loren. And by the way, it's been a real blessing to have a cousin as my pastor. I know it wasn't an accident. I know God placed him in my life at the exact right time.

We talked, and I explained the seriousness of my wife's condition. We prayed for a while. He gave me some prophetic words and reminded me of God's promises and the words spoken over my wife some twenty five years earlier. Those were the first positive words I had heard. As I mentioned previously, my son Tim and his ex Angela, were in the emergency room, so I went back inside to wait. After a while, I decided to find a place where we could pray privately.

I asked if they had a chapel. I knew they did. After all, it was a Catholic hospital. And besides, I think all hospitals have some type of chapel or places to pray. The last time I had gone to a chapel at a hospital to pray was when my dad died, and as you know, the outcome wasn't a positive one. Yes, as I mentioned in chapter 2, my dad had died of a brain aneurysm almost forty years earlier, so you can see in what direction my mind was going.

I couldn't believe this was happening again. I mean, I had prayed before, and it didn't do any good. *Why should this be any different?* I thought. But I knew I was going to find God. I knew I couldn't contain myself any longer, so we headed for the chapel. When we arrived, I actually exploded in prayer. I prayed in the spirit for a long period of time, but inwardly, I understood what I was saying. I didn't even know I was praying in the Spirit until sometime later when I was talking to my son Tim.

After several hours of prayer I knew I had told God everything that was in my heart. Not that He didn't already know, He always knows what's in our hearts. But I realize now that this was the first time I was totally honest about my feelings or what I felt inside. And I was extremely angry.

"After all," I prayed, "are you my Father? Haven't I waited patiently? Haven't I been obedient? Haven't I waited all these years for You to do all the things You said you were going to do?" I was extremely angry and had never dared to approach God, with this type of attitude. Thinking back, it makes me feel a bit uncomfortable, but after all, God knew the emotional stress that I was going through.

As I continued to pray I said, "Remember when I slipped out of bed at night to seek You and You came to me? You held my hand during those critical times of my life, and You continued to visit me for some twenty-five years. Didn't You say You would be my Father and I would be your son? Didn't You say You would never leave me or forsake me? Didn't You say You would give me the desires of my heart?"

As I said previously I don't know how long I prayed. My son Tim and Angela had left, and it was getting light outside.

I prayed until I was interrupted by a nurse telling me the doctor had arrived and needed to talk with me about my wife's condition. The doctor explained my wife's condition extensively. He said the bleeding had not stopped, and he needed to go in immediately to try to repair the rupture. He went on to explain that a shunt had been inserted in the area of the bleed, which I already knew, but I was extremely thankful for his thoroughness. He said her condition was so grave that he couldn't make any promises, but he would do everything he could possibly do.

He said, "Your wife is being prepped for surgery and I need for you to sign a release and consent form." I agreed. Then Dr. Spetzler hurried off to prepare for surgery. He didn't know how long it would take. A short time after the start of surgery, our two sons had arrived from Michigan and asked me for an update. I told them I had not heard anything, and we immediately started to pray and then wait. They waited in the waiting room mostly, but I needed to walk and pray, and I walked and I walked and I prayed. I prayed out loud in the Spirit up and down the halls and in the stairwells, passing people on the way.

Yes, I prayed in the Spirit. People thought I was crazy, but I didn't care. I was not letting go of my wife or God's promises. Looking back, it reminds me of the story of Jacob as he wrestled with God.

Then Jacob was left alone; and a Man wrestled with him until the breaking of day. Now when He saw that He did not prevail against him, He touched the socket of his hip; and the socket of Jacob's hip was out of joint as He wrestled with him. And He said, "Let Me go, for the day breaks." But he said, "I

will not let You go unless You bless me!" So He said to him, "What is your name?"And he said, "Jacob." And He said, "Your name shall no longer be called Jacob, but Israel; for you have struggled with God and with men, and have prevailed." Then Jacob asked Him saying, "Tell me Your name, I pray." And He said, "Why is it that you ask about My name?" And He blessed him there. And Jacob called the name of the place Peniel: "For I have seen God face to face, and my life is preserved." (Genesis 32: 24-30)

I know God has given me a new name because of my persistence during this trial. **(See Rev. 2:17 3:12 and Is. 62:2) "God says, He will give us a new name.")** But at the time, that was not one of my thoughts. I just knew I didn't want to lose my wife.

I can't remember how long the surgery lasted, but I know it was all day. Every few hours, one of the surgeons would come out with an update, and every update got worse. They said it was more extensive than they had anticipated, but they were going to continue with the surgery. We continued to pray. They prayed inwardly, and I walked and prayed outwardly.

There were a lot of people in the waiting room whose relatives were waiting as well. I didn't want to bother them, so I continued to walk and pray. I think ten to twelve hours later, the doctor came to tell me the news. He again explained. It was much worse than he had thought. He said it was the worst bleed he had ever had at that time, and he didn't know what was going to happen because of the extent of the blood in the brain. Keep in mind, Dr. Spetzler is one of the leading brain surgeons in the world and has seen his fair share of brain aneurysms.

Now it was a waiting game. I thought to myself, *maybe I should fast. I'm sure I can get my way if I fast.* I tried fasting, but I couldn't. I had always been able to fast. I didn't understand why, but I knew God didn't want me to fast, so we went to the cafeteria to eat. I had been up for about thirty-six hours or more and hadn't slept or eaten, but I wasn't tired.

After eating, I told my boys they needed to go to the house and get some rest. They weren't fond of that idea, but because of their fatigue, they decided to follow my advice. Well, it wasn't really advice. After all, I am their dad, and they were older now and usually followed my orders. As I told you before, I was used to giving orders. That's who I am. That is my personality, as much as I try to change. It's extremely difficult to change that part of my personality.

The hospital staff informed me that my wife was on full life support, and as soon as she was settled in ICU, I would be able to see her. After a few hours had passed they came and informed me that I could see her. When I walked into the room and saw my wife, I was gripped by fear. There were tubes and wires all over her body and a large one stuck down her throat. I immediately started to sob, but regained my composure quickly. I knew I had to remain calm and have my full faculties in order to make the right decisions.

I didn't leave the hospital that night either. That was my second night, but I still could not sleep. I continued to pray in the waiting room. Yes, on my knees! I had gone to a different waiting room that was empty at the time. I did fall asleep while praying but only for a few minutes. I got up and continued to walk. My wife says pace. I guess I am a pacer, and I don't mean a basketball player either.

My sons Jim and Marc returned to the hospital early the next morning, just after my meeting with Dr. Spetzler. He explained what he had done during the surgery, and explained that while repairing the aneurysm he had seen another aneurysm on the other side of her brain. However, because of the severity of the bleed and the amount of blood, he didn't want to keep her open any longer than he had to. And besides, there was already too much damage. He went on to say, he had never seen that much blood on the brain before.

After a few days, my son Jim had to return home to Michigan. After all, he did have a family to support. Marc stayed on, but by my request, he stayed at the house a great deal of the time to allow me to continue seeking God. The following morning, the chaplain came to get me. She took me into a small office with several chairs, maybe seven or eight, and asked me to sit down at the table, along with several doctors I knew because of the presence of the chaplain and the doctors, that this was not going to be good.

They explained that my wife had suffered two major strokes during the night, and upon a thorough examination, they could not find any activity in her brain. They said I should think about taking her off of life support and letting her go.

My wife and I had talked about this topic many times; I think all husbands and wives discuss this. During those discussions, we both shared with one another that if this ever happened, we would terminate life support. However, I did not share that information with the hospital staff. I told them I would have to pray about it. The chaplain gave me some paperwork to take home and fill out, and she suggested I discuss this matter with the rest of my family. After all, I was so tired. I felt numb and didn't want to make such a critical decision on my own, so I agreed that this would be a good idea.

When I walked into the house that evening, everyone there looked at me and said, "What's wrong?" Now remember, I was going home to discuss termination of life support, but that's not what happened. God said, "Tell them everything is fine," That's what I did, but I felt like I was lying.

Angela had fixed me something to eat. It was delicious, and I went straight to my room. I hadn't been there in days. I got in bed, laid there for a few minutes, and said to myself, "Is this it?" Then I started to cry uncontrollably, and it started to sink in.

The loneliness was deafening. I could actually hear the loneliness. Coming from a family of ten, I was never lonely, and because I was married at a very early age, it didn't allow much time to be lonely. So I started to pray. I told God, everything the hospital had told me, and then I told Him the decision that Karen and I had made about this type of situation (like He didn't already know.) Then I asked for his consent to remove her from life support. He said no! He didn't say anything else, He didn't have to but I didn't understand why. I left it at that.

I finally fell asleep. I didn't know how long I had slept, but when I woke up, I woke up with a start and thought that I had slept all night and all day and it was night again. I didn't know. I knew I was still tired, but that wasn't uncommon. I had undergone heart surgery a short time before and hadn't regained my strength. But soon I realized I had only slept about two hours.

I jumped in the shower, got dressed and hurried off to the hospital. I arrived around daybreak. I went straight to ICU to check on my wife's condition. The nurse asked if I had made any decision about removing Karen from life support, and I told her I had. I told her my decision was to leave Karen on life support, and not only was it my decision but God's decision as well.

She replied, "Almost everyone says that, but it hasn't happened yet. But I would like to say, you are making a terrible mistake. Even if your wife was able to breathe on her own she would be a vegetable or like a baby and you would never be able to care for her."

I said, "That would be my decision not yours."

Then she walked away. I would like to tell you that I had an enormous amount of faith, but that wouldn't be true. What I did have was a tiny bit of faith, and a whole lot of obedience, although I'm not sure in what order.

Chapter 6

THE AWAKENING

After the nurse left the room, I walked over to my wife's bed to talk to her. Even though the hospital staff said she couldn't hear me, I had decided I was going to talk to her as though she could. I went to the right side of the bed to hold her hand because her left hand was paralyzed and in a fist, but as I did, I could see one of her shoulders was dry. I decided to rub some lotion on her shoulder, and as I did, she actually raised her shoulder as I started to rub.

I told the nurse, and she said it was my imagination. She actually came back into the room and started running tests. These tests consisted of taking her knuckles and pressing extremely hard in certain areas of Karen's body to cause a reaction to pain, trying to convince me to let my wife go, or at least that's the way it appeared. I didn't know why the nurse continued running these tests because I had already made up my mind. When my mind's made up, only God can change it.

The nurse even demonstrated my wife's inability to breathe *on* her own. I said thank you, and she left again. She actually had a cubicle in the middle of two patients who were on life support. I visited for a time, and a group of staff members came in and asked me to leave. They have certain procedures they have to perform on the patients, and they don't want you in the way. I went back to the waiting room, and a few hours later, several doctors came in, including Dr. Spetzler, to discuss my wife's condition.

They explained her condition again, like maybe I had forgotten, and after they walked away, Dr. Spetzler came over to talk privately. He said, "I did your wife's surgery. I can't tell you your wife is going to recover. All I can say is, don't give up hope."

I think these were the first words of encouragement from a doctor. I said, "Thank you very much," and he left hurriedly. He seemed to always be in a hurry, understandably so. A short time later, the chaplain came to see me and again asked me if I had made any decisions.

I said, "Yes, I have made my decision. The answer is no, I'm not taking her off life support."

She said, "Why!"

I said, "Because God said so,"

She said, "You're kidding yourself." Again she reminded me that lots of people had told her this and it hadn't happened yet. Then she said, "You know leaving her on life support is not going to make any difference."

I said, "Okay! If it's not going to make any difference, let's leave her on life support." She said okay, and that was it.

These were very difficult times for me because I had no one to talk to, or so I thought. Looking back, I realize this was a time that I used to develop a closer relationship with God. However, I did stay in contact with family members, and my pastor in Michigan. He sent me a miracle cloth from my aunt Jean (Respectfully known as Mama Jean). Every day I would go into Karen's room, hold the cloth on different parts of my wife's body, and pray for a healing.

Like always, I do most of the talking, but when I take time to listen, that's when the changes come. Not in me alone, but in everyone I come in contact with.

And He said to them, "Take heed what you hear. With the same measure you use, it will be measured to you; and to you who hear, more will be given." (Mark 4:24)

Then Paul stood up, and motioning with his hand said, "Men of Israel, and you who fear God, listen. (Acts 13:16)

Having eyes, do you not see? And having ears, do you not hear? And do you not remember? (Mark 8:18)

I know now if we take the time to listen to God, He will guide us to a new destination in Him. Day after day, with very little faith, I continued on with no good news. Day after day, I continued to seek God, but I still remembered the statements made about my wife. Those statements were, "She will never be the same person. She will never be able to make her own decisions. She will be totally dependent. She will never walk on her own or have her own thoughts."

I am not sure why, but everyone seemed so negative, with the exception of a very few. Maybe it was because of the type of facility, or environment or the recovery rate of most brain injuries. Even though our medical advancements in brain surgery have come so far since my dad's death from an aneurysm. And Barrow Neurological Center, along with Dr. Spetzler from what I understand is one of the leaders in that field. However, the recovery rate of these brain trauma patients is still extremely poor.

Even though my life was in crisis, I made some friends at the hospital, doctors, nurses, and often times the relatives of patients who were in crisis just like I was. This hospital was extremely busy. People or patients were flying in from all over the world, and it seemed as though the helicopter landed about every two minutes, but in reality it was more like forty-five minutes to an hour. We all had something in common, and we all seemed to bond at a certain level. Many came and left while I was there. some of the outcomes were good, and some weren't.

As I mentioned earlier, I made lots of friends at the hospital, and some of these were the ones that didn't survive. Keep in mind their diagnoses were nowhere near the severity of my wife's. After twenty-nine days, not one person was there in the ICU who was there when I got there. It seemed they would be there one day and gone the next. (I mean really gone.)

As my fatigue continued to grow and my decision making abilities started to diminish, and because I had promised my wife that I would never allow her to live like that. After twenty-nine days (with no more answers from God concerning my wife) I decided to remove my wife from life support. It was a decision that didn't come easily, but with no improvement, I thought maybe I hadn't heard what I thought I had heard from God. (I know all of us question our ability to hear from God at certain times of our life.)

I left the hospital and went home to share this decision with the rest of the family. But for some reason, I still couldn't bring myself to tell them about my decision, so I took a shower, got cleaned up, and headed back to the hospital.

On the way there, I looked over on the seat, and there was a CD my son Jim had sent me. It was a mix of praise and worship music that I hadn't listened to yet. I thought to myself, *"The least I can do is listen to this CD"*. *After all, he did take the time to put it together.* I reached over and slid the CD in. Remember, even though I had continued to seek God all these years, my worship and praise hadn't been very consistent, and lacked intimacy at times.

However, as I began to worship and praise, almost immediately I was ushered into a place I hadn't been in a long time. I was in the presence of God, actually in the throne room. I had been there before, but had never asked for anything. I was always so overwhelmed by His presence I could never think of anything to say. Although, I know that every time I am ushered into His presence, I am changed. This time it was different, I had plenty to say. I immediately felt the love, peace and joy of His embrace. It was extremely familiar, and I had almost forgotten how wonderful it was to be in His Glory presence.

Then He said, "Jimmie, I have missed your worship and praise, so ask Me what you will."

I know He already knew what I wanted; He just wanted me to ask.(Now remember, I was on my way back to the hospital to remove my wife from life support.) I said, "Lord, I will give You everything I have if You will give me my wife back."

He said, "You don't have anything. Everything you have is already mine."

I said, "Yes, Father. I have forgotten."

He said, "Yes, I know! But I am going to give your wife back to you as a free gift. And I want nothing in return except your worship and praise."

I said, "Lord, You will have my worship and praise from now on, regardless of the outcome or circumstances. But Father, the doctors said my wife doesn't have the ability to recover."

He said, "I can do whatever I wish. Always remember, everything that was made I made, including your wife, I do remember every promise that I have made to you, and every promise will be delivered."

Then it was over, but because of my mental, physical, and emotional fatigue I was sure I had been hallucinating. I understand now how sleep deprivation can affect the human mind so negatively. After all, I had almost been convinced that I had lost my mind and was too fatigued to make any rational decisions. I continued my drive to the hospital.

When I got to the hospital, I went to my wife's room to say my goodbyes. I went to her right side to hold her good hand and talk to her. As I laid my head on the bed and wept, I thought about the great love we had shared for one another and how I would miss the touch of her hand in mine. I was even wondering if I could continue without her. I couldn't even think about how much I would miss her, and lo and behold, she started rubbing my head, startled. I looked up, and my wife's eyes were open. She was awake.

I immediately went to the nurse and said, "My wife is awake." I realize now this was God's appointed time, and He knew exactly how long I would wait. **(Isaiah 40:31) says, "But those who wait on the LORD Shall renew their strength; They shall mount up with wings like eagles, They shall run and not be weary, They shall walk and not faint."**

The nurse said "That's not possible," and she came directly into the room. She said, "Oh my God, I guess she is." She asked me to leave so she could work on my wife. I agreed and went to the waiting room and called my son Marc to tell him the news.

Angela, my son Tim's ex drove him to the hospital. Shortly after their arrival, the nurse came to the waiting room and said I could come back in. I went in to the room, and a great deal of equipment had been removed. I asked if Marc and Angela could come in, the nurse said yes and she would get them. When they entered the room, the nurse walked over to my son, Marc, placed her hand on his shoulder, and said, "Is this your daughter?"

Karen said, well she couldn't speak because her throat was paralyzed, but she shook her head yes. Then the nurse went to Angela and said, "Is this your son?" Then again Karen shook her head yes.

Then the nurse looked at me and said, "I told you so," You see, this was the nurse who was so insistent that my wife wouldn't recover, and when I realized that my wife didn't know anybody I said inwardly with panic, "Oh God! I think we made a mistake."

God said, "I don't make mistakes."

I know now Karen didn't even know the difference between yes and no. The following day, my wife was moved to another floor because they said she didn't need to be in ICU any longer. The new floor that she was transferred to was almost as amazing as the ICU. They had cameras in almost every location of the room, or so it appeared, and I could only visit for a few minutes at a time. However I was extremely thankful for the thoroughness of their care.

I was still extremely tired and very excited about her awakening but still very concerned about Karen's inability to recognize people and objects. It was as though she was a baby, and I became very protective of her and felt like I couldn't leave her side. This became a problem later on, because when anyone would ask her a question, I would answer for her. But she quickly reminds me that she has a mind of her own and can certainly answer for herself.

Chapter 7

REHAB.

Karen was on that new floor for only one day for observation and was then transferred to the rehabilitation facility right at the hospital. Even though Karen was awake, I'm quite certain she didn't know anyone. I was pretty sure she didn't know me either. I could tell by the way she looked at me. This was extremely difficult, and it troubled me deeply.

After a few days, I could tell she was starting to bond with me again. Even though she couldn't talk, I could feel a strong connection between us, and so could the rest of the hospital staff, as they mentioned to me on numerous occasions. My son Marc had returned home to Michigan, and I felt very alone.

The truth of the matter was, I was not totally convinced I had made the right decision. Could they have been right? Karen, after being tested, had the intelligence and maturity of a three-year-old. When she was asked questions, she would respond by shaking her head yes or no. Elaine, her speech therapist, would pick up an object such as a comb, and would say, "Is this a window?" My wife would respond by shaking her head yes. This was extremely saddening. After all, I know I had said I would be able to care for my wife, but Karen couldn't even perform the simplest of tasks. I didn't realize how difficult her care would be.

Many times, I said, "Lord, did we make a mistake?" I said we because I asked Him to give me my wife back regardless of her condition. He didn't say anything, or maybe He did and I wasn't listening. I was still extremely tired and didn't want to leave the hospital. At that point, because of my fatigue and frustration, I decided not to go into the room during speech therapy. I stayed outside the room, sat in a chair, and prayed.

On around the third day, about forty-five minutes into therapy, as I recall, Elaine burst from the room and exclaimed, "You're not going to believe this! Your wife has gone from a three-year-old level to a fifth grade level in forty-five minutes."

We were ecstatic, and at that point in time, I was starting to realize, more and more each day, that God's words were true. Sometimes we doubt ourselves. There were times when I thought I was losing my mind, and I guess I was. My wife could whisper in my ear, and I could understand what she was saying she couldn't talk audibly but whispered frequently, and with her fingers, she would motion to me to come close so she could whisper to me.

Even though my wife was starting to improve, there were a great many things she had to relearn, and I was trying to teach her, especially things concerning our life together. I explained that we have three children, three boys. One lived in Arizona, and two lived in Michigan. I explained that they were grown and had been there but had returned home to Michigan to their families. She immediately motioned to me to come close and asked, "Do we have grandchildren?"

I said, "Yes we do." We have six grandchildren.

I decided it was time to bring one of them to the hospital, his name is Joshua. He was the oldest and lived in Arizona, and he was extremely close to his grandmother. Furthermore, his younger brother Darian, was not old enough to understand. Besides, the other grandchildren lived in Michigan.

Now remember, my wife still had no control over her body. Her left arm, right leg, and throat were still paralyzed, and she still had a feeding tube in her nose and a shunt to drain the fluid from her brain. This was because of the ICP's or inner cranial pressure, which was extremely high. Each day I would dress her, pick her up, put her in a wheelchair, and tie her in with a sheet to keep her from falling out. I didn't mind at all. I would take her to the gym for physical therapy, and that day in particular was when Joshua was coming to visit.

You see, the reason I chose Joshua was because of his age and something he said to me when I came home to shower one day, a week or so into her coma. When I opened the door, he ran to me and said, "Grandpa, God wants you to know that Grandma is going to be fine." This came at a time when I really needed a word of encouragement, and these words helped me to continue on.

He came in to see his Grandma with a book in his hand, you know those books they use to teach children their ABCs. He went straight to her without hesitation, got up on her lap, looked straight into her eyes, and said, "Grandma, I am going to teach you your ABCs, and I'm going to be real patient with you, just like you were with me."

This was because I had already explained to him that his grandmother had forgotten almost everything. So he sat on her lap at a table and proceeded to teach her the ABCs. It only took a few minutes, and she was actually writing them. This was around the same time as her therapist Elaine had started working with her. I thought, *"Wow something is going on inside of her."* I was so excited, to say the least.

As Karen's therapist continued working with her, she was learning so fast I couldn't believe it. However, there were still days that were extremely difficult. I think it was because of my fatigue and her grueling schedule. I would get Karen up, brush her teeth, wash her, or give her a shower. I even shaved her legs several times. But because I hadn't been going home and was staying right at the hospital, I still hadn't slept, except for an occasional nap. I was extremely tired, and everyone told me so, like I really needed to be reminded.

A short time into rehab, I was approached by some of the hospital staff. They said, "You should go home and get some rest, shower, shave, and then return." Reluctantly, I agreed, even though I didn't feel comfortable leaving my wife. I thought, "*I do need to shower.*" I left, but when I returned, two or three hours later, my wife wasn't in her room.

I immediately went to the nurse's station, to ask where my wife was, and they explained. Someone had forgotten to tie my wife down in her straitjacket, and one of the staff informed me she had been taken to get an M.R.I. The nurse explained that Karen had fallen headfirst on the cement floor and was unconscious. I thought, "*Someone's getting choked.*" That's not really exactly what I thought; only God knows. Besides, when I get angry, my vocabulary isn't always what it should be. After all, this was my wife, and I felt somewhat responsible for leaving her side. I wouldn't want anyone to know exactly what my thoughts were at that time. I would be embarrassed.

Within a few minutes, they brought my wife back from x-ray and informed me there was no damage, although I'm not so sure. It seemed as though she had regressed slightly, but I knew I would never leave her side again. After all, I promised her dad I would never leave her side.

In spite of this incident, my wife's progress was astounding. I couldn't believe that she was learning so rapidly. I could see God's intervention, but each day was a new day. It was one day at a time. Actually, it was minute by minute. I can remember one day I was standing by her bedside, which I did for hours at a time, and at that time, she still had a feeding tube in her nose. It ran up her nose, down her throat, and into her stomach.

I hadn't been there very long. I looked at her, and she still had her straitjacket on and was tied down. I thought, "*I can't stand this any longer. I'm going to untie her.*" I said, "Sweetheart, if you will promise not to pull the tube out of your nose. I will un tie you. Will you promise?" She responded by nodding her head yes, so I undid her straitjacket and removed one arm, and while I was removing the other arm, I looked, and the tube was out. She looked at me like, "Got you."

You see, this wasn't the first time. It was actually getting comical, but not to the hospital staff. Every time that this would happen they had to take her to surgery and reinsert the tube. Then again later, after she returned from surgery, I thought, "*I can't stand here any longer. I'm getting tired. I'm going to lay in bed with her.* After the tube was reinserted and they brought her back, that's exactly what I did.

Every time the nurses would walk by, they would say, "You can't lay in bed with the patient."

I would respond by saying, "Okay," and after a while, I would just smile. But sometimes when I was extremely tired and cross, I would say, "Call the bed police."

Besides, I didn't know how anyone could sleep. The helicopters were coming and going so frequently it seemed like every couple of minutes especially while I was sleeping or trying to sleep. But things were starting to get better, and after a while, most of the staff would just walk by and smile back at me. After a while, hardly anybody said anything.

Like I mentioned before, things were starting to happen, but what I didn't realize was that the miracles had just begun. My spiritual growth and intimacy with God was growing so rapidly. Know I was starting to realize more and more what a mighty God we have and how much He loves us.

For God so loved the world that He gave His ONLY begotten SON, that whoever believes in Him should not perish but have everlasting life. (John 3:16)

Who shall separate us from the love of Christ? Shall tribulation, or distress or persecution, or famine or nakedness, or peril, or sword? (Romans 8:35)

Yet in all these things we are more than conquerors through Him who loved us. For I am persuaded that neither death nor life, nor angels nor principalities nor powers, nor things present nor things to come, nor height nor depth, nor any other created thing, shall be able to separate us from the love of God which is in Christ Jesus our Lord.(Romans 8:37-39)

My hope and prayers are that all who read this book will understand how much God loves them. There are no exceptions to this, so when someone tries to tell you that you have to earn God's love, don't believe it. I know there will be things you will want to do for God, and it will give you more blessings, but remember, God already loves you passionately.

As we exercise our faith, it will grow stronger, and our works will **increase. (James 2:18) says, But someone will say, "You have faith, and I have works."** Show me your faith without your works, and I will show you my faith by my works. We will find more favor with God, and our love for Him will grow, but His love for us won't. God has already demonstrated His love for us when He sent His only Son, Jesus Christ to die on the cross for us.

Chapter 8

MIRACLES

The question is, does God still do miracles today? I'm here to tell you that He does, and I'm going to share a few of those miracles with you. You see, I've always been extremely skeptical and had a very difficult time believing that God still works miracles today. After all, I've been told by many pastors that God doesn't do miracles today and that God only used the original twelve disciples or apostles to perform these miracles.

**And these signs will follow those who believe: In my name they will cast out demons; they will speak with new tongues; they will take up serpents; and if they drink anything deadly, it will by no means hurt them; they will lay hands on the sick, and they will recover."
(Mark 16: 17-18)**

Now concerning spiritual gifts, brethren, I do not want you to be ignorant: But the manifestation of the spirit is given to each one for the profit of all: For to one is given the word wisdom through the spirit, to another the word of knowledge through the same spirit, to another faith by the same spirit, to another

> **gifts of healing by the same spirit, to another the working of miracles, to another prophecy, to another discerning of spirits, to another different kinds of tongues, to another the interpretation of tongues. But one and the same spirit works all these things, distributing to each one individually as He wills. (1 Corinthians 12:1, 7–11)**

As you can see, God is still going to use His children to do miracles today to accomplish His will.

It seemed as though each day, or even each hour, brought miracles while Karen was in the hospital. Every time it happened, it caused my faith to grow. Sometimes I felt like an idiot. Other people would watch as I rubbed the miracle cloth on my wife's body, praying for a healing. At first the process was slow, but then started to gain momentum. After a while I was beginning to think I could walk on water. (Just joking)

As I mentioned in the previous chapter, every day I would pick my wife up, put her in a wheelchair, tie her in, and take her to the gym. At first I could only watch, but as I listened to God, He started giving me instructions. I know, you're probably thinking, *who does this guy think he is? God doesn't speak to people today.* I have news for you: not only does our God do miracles today; He does still speak to us.

Keep in mind when God speaks to you that it needs to line up with His Word and His personality. I have heard some people say God told them to do something, but when they told me what it was, I knew it wasn't from God. To be quite honest with you, I have made that same mistake myself. After a while, I realized it was me talking to me. Remember, we need to use some common sense, and remember, God will never tell you to do anything contrary to His Word. Always talk to your pastor or an elder to make sure, especially during crisis situations, that you are hearing from God.

I'm not saying He always speaks to us audibly. Most of the time God speaks to our inner man, and the reason He speaks to our inner man is because He has taken up residence in us **(Luke17:20-21). Now when He was asked by the Pharisees when the kingdom of God would come, He answered them and said, "The kingdom of God does not come with observation; "nor will they say, 'See here! Or see there!' For indeed, the kingdom of God is within you."**

As we were sitting in the gym and I was listening to God, I saw a large ball. Remember, my wife was tied in a wheelchair and only had the use of her right hand and left leg. God said, "Jimmie, pick up the ball and toss it to your wife. "I thought, *Lord, I don't think this is a very good idea*, but I was obedient. I picked up the ball and tossed it to her very lightly. The ball hit her right in the face. If looks could kill, I'm sure I wouldn't be here today. This was also the first time I had seen any type of emotion from Karen.

I felt very sorry and stupid at the same time. It seemed as though everyone was watching, and the Lord said, "Do it again." I picked up the ball and tossed it ever so lightly, and she put up her arm to prevent the ball from hitting her again. Then as I continued tossing the ball to her, around the tenth time, she started catching it. Even though her left hand wasn't working, she was able to catch the ball and throw it back.

One of the therapists who had been watching was starting to take interest and wanted to start working with her, which was great for me. But Karen had no use of her left hand, and as hard as the therapist worked, it didn't seem to make any difference. Karen was still unable to move her hand. I grabbed the miracle cloth, rubbed it on my wife's hand, and said, "In Jesus' name, be healed," and almost immediately, she started using her hand. However, because she hadn't used it for such a long period of time, it was very weak, and she was extremely uncoordinated.

I thought, *Wow, this is cool.* Because of my obedience, my faith was starting to grow. It was extremely difficult for me to step out and make these statements of healing, and if you know me, you know it had to be God working through me. I almost always have the thought, *What if I say these things in front of people, and it doesn't happen?* But I think all of us have these thoughts.

The next day, the therapist started working to strengthen Karen's hand, and I continued to work with my wife as well. That day was another miracle day, sort of like a tidal wave. We were in the gym, and I turned on some music. It was from the 60's now keep in mind Karen and I were married in 1965. The 60's were when my wife and I met, and we both loved to dance. When the music started, I glanced at my wife, and it appeared as though she was trying to snap her fingers. I asked God inwardly, "Lord, what should I do?"

He said, "Pick your wife up and dance with her!"

Remember, my wife at that time only weighed around seventy pounds and seemed very fragile. She seemed as light as a feather that day. I went to her wheelchair, untied Karen, and started to dance with her. At first both of her feet hung limply. Keep in mind because of the location of her aneurysm and her two strokes; her right leg was still paralyzed. But I knew that I had already placed the miracle cloth on her leg and asked God to heal it, and my confidence in what He could do was continuing to grow.

Within a matter of minutes, my wife started moving both legs and was starting to put weight on both legs. Then one of the physical therapists walked over and asked, "Would you mind if I worked with your wife?"

I said, "Not at all."

I thought to myself *Isn't this his job?* But anyway, he motioned for me to bring Karen over to an area that had two railings for her to hold on to. I helped her onto the rails, stood behind her, and held her by the waist with my hands so she wouldn't fall. After a few minutes, my wife was able to do it on her own. I could see the determination on her face, and I felt a great deal of gratification. There were still a lot of problems, but each day Karen was continuing to progress!

One of the biggest problems was the feeding tube and her continued weight loss. One of her doctors approached me about inserting a feeding tube into her side. He said it would probably be a permanent thing because her throat was paralyzed. He went on to explain, when she swallow's her food, it is going into her lungs. He then asked for consent to perform the procedure. I immediately grabbed the miracle cloth, rubbed it on her neck and throat, and said, "In Jesus' name, be healed."

The doctors looked at each other, and then looked at me as if to say, "What a nut." I told the doctor I wanted her checked again. He said, "We just checked her this morning, and it's not going to make any difference."

I said, "It's my money. Check her again.

He said, "I'll check her on one condition: if you'll come into x-ray and watch the results for yourself." I agreed, and he said, "I'll call and make the necessary arrangements."

About an hour later, they came to her room to get us. We went to x-ray, and they tied her in a seat. They gave her some type of food that looked like baby food. I guess it had some type of dye or radioactive isotopes in it. I'm not sure if that's right, but I think I'm close.

When the nurse gave her a bite, the doctor said, "I want you to come over here and look for yourself. You will see the food going into her lungs."

I said okay, and he said, "See!" Then he said, "Oh my God! Her throat is perfectly normal."

I didn't say anything, but I know they could see the gratification on my face. I wanted to say, "God can do anything," but I didn't. What a faith builder that was, not just for me but for everyone involved.

But we were not out of the woods yet. For some reason, my wife refused to eat. I couldn't understand why, so I asked the doctors. (*Oh, by the way*, you should see her eat now; it's actually a thing of beauty.) They said it was very common for patients to refuse to eat after this type of brain trauma. No matter what I did, she wouldn't eat. However, I knew if she refused to eat, she would still require the insertion of a feeding tube in her side.

They recommended I bring her down to rehab, to eat with the other patients. She sat down at the table and started to eat. The only problem was, she was eating off the tray of the person next to her. I said, "Honey, you need to eat your own food. That's his food."

She responded, "That's too much food for him to eat."

We all started laughing, but the person whose food she was eating didn't think it was funny. The next day we went down to the eating area. She sat down by the same person, and he started cramming food in his mouth. The nurse stood abruptly, and said, "Hey! Why are you doing that? Why are you eating so fast?"

He said, pointing at my wife, "I'm trying to keep up with her."

I couldn't help but laugh again. As you can see, we were learning, or I was learning, to deal with these problems with some humor. Each day my wife continued to grow stronger. I worked with her every day after the therapists were done. She had this belt they had given her. It was called a gait belt, and I would put it on her and walk her up and down the hall until she would let me know she was tired.

We would also work on her memory, and her progress was amazing. Within two weeks, the hospital staff called me in to the office and said, "We don't believe there's anything more we can do for your wife. We think your wife is ready to go home. But because of her ICPs, we will have to insert a permanent shunt into her head to drain that area of the brain to prevent pressure from building up."

I thought, *they don't know my wife. She would never tolerate that type of situation.* The shunt was going to run under her skin in her scalp all the way to her throat, down her throat, and into her stomach, and it would have to be cleaned out occasionally. I took out the miracle cloth, put it on my wife's head, and started to pray. The really strange thing was that this time when I prayed, I actually knew what was going to happen. Now every time Karen and I pray together, we know that the things we pray about are going to happen and can actually see changes almost immediately.

When I was finished, I said, "I want you to check my wife's ICPs." This time they agreed without argument, but insisted no one with that type of bleed had ever left without a shunt to drain and relieve pressure. After checking the pressure, to their amazement it had returned to normal.

This new tool or weapon that God has given us has been absolutely incredible. I don't know if these gifts could have ever happened without this aneurysm or even if this ministry could have grown out of any other circumstances. It's hard to believe that after thirty years, God has given us this ministry together. We call it Miracle Ministries, which was a name that took us months to come up with. Even then, we know it was God who came up with this name.

When we came up with this name, we were visiting in Michigan, and had gone to Mount Zion our home church. As we were walking out of the service, an old friend asked how we were doing. We confided that we were starting a new ministry, and he asked, "What is the name of your ministry?"

I immediately responded, "Miracle Ministries."

That was a name I had not even contemplated or thought of up to that point, and if you knew me, you would know that name didn't come from me. And besides, how could God possibly use someone like me to build His kingdom? Karen and I are starting to realize that God's timing is absolutely perfect. His kingdom will come in its time, but it's our job to listen and prepare for this glorious visitation.

A few days later, against all odds and against hospital policy, Karen walked out of the hospital. But because of her instability, I walked beside her and held onto her. The hospital staff applauded. It felt so wonderful to be taking my wife home. This was something I thought I would never experience. After all, she went from no chance for survival to riding next to me in the car, but this adventure had just begun. Yes, I call it an adventure. Our life now is a wonderful adventure with one another in Christ. So remember, you men, if you are reading this, whenever your wife wants to talk to you and you don't want to listen, think about this incident. Always remember your life together could be over in the blink of an eye.

Chapter 9

COMING HOME

It was so wonderful having my wife at home. I had almost forgotten or even had never really appreciated being able to have my wife at home. There was still a lot of work to be done and a great deal of outpatient therapy. The injuries caused by the aneurysm and two strokes were still very apparent.

Karen had lost most of her decision making abilities and I had to watch her very closely. Her small motor skills had not developed yet. Small tasks, like tying her shoes and fastening her buttons, were a real chore for her. Bathing was almost always a two hour process. I started doing all the cooking, cleaning, and banking, which was not my strong suit. Karen, because of her knowledge in banking and finance, had always taken care of these tasks.

Karen would start a project, forget what she was doing and go on to another project. To this day, she still has a difficult time completing a project with one exception her unquenchable desire, for a personal relationship with God and a great desire to establish His kingdom.

She was like having another child at first, but every day I could see small improvements. She thought she could do everything on her own. I can remember trying to help her.

It reminded me of my boys when they were growing up. They wanted to do everything on their own, even when they couldn't

I think it's our nature to want to do things on our own. That's why it can be difficult to trust God. Because Karen was like a child, I would allow her to try things on her own before giving her help. Does this remind you of anyone? It reminds me of how our desire for independence from God causes us to get in trouble.

I want you to think about this for a minute. When we exclude God from our decision-making, I believe we exalt ourselves above God. But as the scales fall from our eyes, we will see ourselves for who we are and seek God for change.

Let no one deceive you by any means; for that day will not come unless the falling away comes first, and the man of sin is revealed, the son of perdition [I believe this is talking about us who opposes and exalts himself above all that is called God or that is worshiped, so that he sits as God in the temple of God, showing himself that he is God. (2 Thess.2:3-4)

Now I know that this is not talking about the coming of the Lord Jesus Christ bodily. This is talking about us and how the scales must fall from our eyes, just as they fell from Paul's eyes at Damascus in **(Acts 9:-18,) "Immediately there fell from his eyes something like scales, and he received his sight at once; and he arose and was baptized."**

I know, in addition to this, God is also talking about the fact that the scales need to fall from our eyes, so that we can see Him. **(First Corinthians 13:12) say's "For now we see in** a mirror, dimly, but then face to face. Now I know in part, but then I shall know just as I also am known."

(Second Thessalonians 2:6) goes on to say, "And now you know what is restraining, that He may be revealed in his own time." Who will be revealed? Christ will be revealed. Where will He be revealed? He will be revealed in us. Furthermore, if we don't see ourselves first and seek Him for change it will be extremely difficult to recognize his visitation.

Keep in mind, in **(John 1:11) it says, "He came to His own, and His own did not receive Him."** This is because sometimes we've already made up our mind about whom and what He is. I believe His people still have this problem. This is before the scales start falling away from our eyes, and that this is an ongoing process.

Always be open for a new revelation or visitation from God. We need to realize we can't do it on our own. Even in the garden, we chose to eat of the tree of the knowledge of good and evil, as opposed to the tree of life, which was Jesus Christ. Oh, we can do some things on our own. I'm not talking about practical things that God has given us dominion over, but the big things remain in His hands.

Okay, back to the story! Therapy was every other day, although it was every day for me. Karen worked diligently to overcome her disabilities. After a period of time, she decided she was going to return to work. I tried to explain to her that she wasn't ready to return to work, but she wouldn't listen. We argued for several days, and I finally realized I couldn't win this battle. I decided to let her return to work, even though she couldn't drive.

Every day, we would get up; I would help her get ready, and drive her to work. Then I would go home, work around the house, and go back and pick her up. It was a minimum of four hours a day. Keep in mind that my wife had aspired to a fairly high position at her job. She had become a mortgage underwriting supervisor. Even though while she was off, they had placed someone else in her position, they allowed her to come back at her former position.

After a few days, they were beginning to realize she had no idea what she was doing. It was at that time I received a call from someone at her work. They told me that my wife was going to be fired because of her inability to perform her job duties. This decision was made long before her return to work. They went on to say, it would not have mattered what her job performance was.

Because of her childlike trust, she couldn't comprehend what was about to take place. When I would go to pick Karen up from work, I would ask her how she was doing and she would say she was doing great. In her eyes, she was doing great, but she didn't realize she couldn't do the job.

After a few more days, another person from her work called, to talk. He explained that the individual who had replaced my wife was a friend of the boss and was not going to step down. They were making plans to fire Karen and had already set these plans in motion. This was another confirmation of what I already knew.

I would try to talk to my wife about this, but she refused to listen, so I decided to call her doctor, Dr. Sally Alcott. I explained the situation to her, and she exclaimed, "Your wife has not been cleared to return to work. And because of her disabilities, she will never return to work."

She told me to come by the office, and she would give me all the necessary paperwork, so I did. I immediately went to Karen's work and presented this paperwork to her boss. I think she was relieved. I believe she was a good person and didn't want to fire Karen, but because of the pressure from higher ups, she was continuing to pursue that course of action.

I got a box, packed up all of Karen's things, and took her home. I know she was relieved but didn't want to admit she couldn't do her job. As it turned out, it worked out in our favor because of her disability insurance. If she would've been fired, she would not have received her benefits. It was a private insurance disability policy, not Social Security disability.

Even though her doctor and all the other doctors involved with my wife's medical condition supplied all documentation, the insurance company refused payment. I don't know if this is a common practice, but it seems to me if you paid a premium, they should honor their commitment to you. After a long battle, lots of prayer, and thousands of dollars in attorney fees, they agreed to pay her disability. I now often wonder, how some people, faced with the same problem can afford to retain an attorney.

As days went by, I could actually see Karen's growth, not just physically and mentally, but equally as important, spiritually. It was almost like the sound of rushing wind, and it was sometimes difficult to contain my excitement. After all, this is the same person who didn't want much to do with God.

You see, when my wife was young, before she met me, she had taught Sunday school. I believe God was bringing all those things back to her remembrance, although I'm not sure about that. Personally I think God taught her while she was in a coma. All I knew was that she had more knowledge about God's word than a great deal of other Christians that I had met.

I started to remember the things that God had spoken to me some thirty years earlier. One of those things in particular was how God had called me to the ministry. I was extremely excited, and studied and read everything I could. I really thought I was ready, and one day, when I was seeking God for direction and telling him I was ready, He spoke very clearly. He stated, "You will be ready when your wife is ready."

I never told anyone about this word. Anyhow, approximately three months after Karen had come home from the hospital, I was working in the garage, and my wife came out. She said, "God wants me to tell you I am ready."

Not remembering the words God had spoken to me thirty years earlier, I responded, "Ready for what?" Then I immediately remembered what God had spoken to me. I almost passed out and started seeking God immediately. I said, "But Father, I think we've waited too long, and now it's too late. Don't you see I'm too old?"

Then later on God spoke to me again. He said, "Jimmie, I want you to read **(Matthew 20:1-16)** I'm not putting all of this in here because it's too long. However, I will use the Scriptures that pertain to this story. This is the parable of the workers in the vineyard and how they were complaining about their reward for their work. I responded, "But Father, you know I've read that many times.

Then He said, "But this time it will have a new meaning."

So being obedient, I read that Scripture.

They said, "These last men have worked only one hour, and You have made them equal to us who have borne the burden and the heat of the day.' "But He answered one of them and said, 'Friend, I am doing you no wrong.

Did you not agree with Me for a denarius?
'Take what is yours and go your way. I wish to
give to this last the same as to you."(Matthew
20:12-14)

Then I said< "Lord, I don't understand."

He said, "Jimmie, "I am going to allow you to work in My vineyard (My Kingdom) for your last hour." And your reward will be the same as those who started at the beginning."

Then I said "Lord, I don't know if I have what it takes."

He said, "Jimmie, you have lots of weaknesses, in fact more than most. And that is where people will see my glory. Remember, I see people differently than the world does. I look at a man's heart. And I have always known that you have a heart after My own. Because of your large family, you have always felt rejected, and that this has caused you to make all those mistakes. I used your mistakes to mold you into what I needed you to be, to help establish My kingdom."

This is not just a kingdom that you get to go to when you die. It is a kingdom, or a spiritual place, that we can go to right here on earth. **(Matthew 19:28) Jesus said, "Assuredly I say to you, that in the regeneration, when the Son of Man sits on the throne of His glory, you who have followed Me will also sit on twelve thrones, judging the twelve tribes of Israel."**

Remember, the disciples didn't die when Jesus did, so these thrones are right here on earth. These thrones are a place of peace and joy in the Holy Spirit, even in the midst of our turmoil and strife. Although I know there is a place we will go to when we die called heaven, I also know He wants us to walk in that realm now when we can walk in unity together, putting aside some of these minor differences, remembering that all of us are in different spiritual places.

We all need to remember this prayer. **(Matthew 6:9-13) In this manner, therefore, pray. Our Father in heaven, Hallowed be Your name. Your kingdom come. Your will be done on earth as it is in heaven. Give us this day our daily bread. And forgive us our debts, As we forgive our debtors. And do not lead us into temptation, But deliver us from the evil one. For Yours is the kingdom and the power and the glory forever. Amen.** God says, "My kingdom will come on earth, just as it is in heaven."More importantly, we need to remember that we must have forgiveness for one another, even in advance. And when God's kingdom is established (and you notice I say when because God's kingdom will be established), we will" come together in unity. Most importantly, we must have love for one another. This is not the love that the world talks about. Sometimes I think even God's people get confused. I'm talking about the kind of love that can only come from God. One day Karen and I were reading the King James Version, and we came across a verse containing the word charity:

> **And though I have the gift of prophecy, and understand all mysteries, and all knowledge, and though I have all faith, so that I could remove mountains, and have not charity, I am nothing And though I bestow all my goods to feed the poor, and though I give my body to be burned and have not charity, it profiteth me nothing. (1 Cor.13: 2-3)**

It didn't make sense, so we decided to look up the word charity in the dictionary. We used the **Webster's New World Dictionary Fourth Edition Michael Agnes Editor in Chief**

Copyright 2003 by Wiley Publishing, Inc. Cleveland Ohio page 111, says, "love for one's fellow human beings, leniency in judging others, generosity toward the needy" The New Merriam-Webster Dictionary Editor in Chief Frederick C. Mish Copyright 1989 by Merriam-Webster Inc. Springfield Massachusetts page 137 says, "good will toward or love of humanity"[1]This didn't make sense. Why would God mention giving all your goods to the poor and then mention charity again? **(Again in 1 Corinthians 13:13) he says, "And now abideth faith, hope, and charity, these three; but the greatest of these is charity."** That's because God is saying we need to have love for humanity. I am sorry, this is not a suggestion; it's a commandment.

> **A new commandment I give to you, that you love one another; as I have loved you, that you also love one another. By this all will know that you are My disciples, if you have love for one another. (John 13: 34-35)**

Is this simple or what? It has to be simple for me or I wouldn't be able to understand. And besides, God doesn't say you are saved by your intelligence. Over thousands of years, scholars have tried to tell us what the Bible said. This has taken God's people to places they didn't need to go. As well intentioned as these people are, they don't realize only the Holy Spirit can give us the understanding we were meant to have.

> **(Proverbs 3:5) says, Trust in the Lord with all of your heart, And lean not on your own understanding." (John 5: 20) says, "And we know that the Son of God has come and has**

1

given us understanding." (John 6:63) says, "It is the spirit who gives life; the flesh profits nothing. The words I speak to you are Spirit, and they are life."

The more I seek God for understanding, the more I understand. The more I understand, the more I seek God. If God gave us all the understanding we needed today, we wouldn't seek Him tomorrow. That's why He only lets us know what's happening on a need to know basis. Furthermore, I would like to say, I believe we should be cautious in our studies, and remember it's God who gives the increase through the Holy Spirit. Let's face it we all know people that can quote every Scripture and have read thousands of books but have very few fruits. I know at times I have been one of those people.

Okay, now you know why it took God all those years to prepare me for the ministry and why He continues to prepare me.

Chapter 10

PREPARING FOR THE MINISTRY

A short time after the garage incident, Karen approached me again. She asked me if we could start looking for a church to attend. I had attended lots of churches in the area, but I hadn't found a church. It wasn't because these churches were not good churches, but I think you will all agree that God has to draw you to a church. The way you can tell if this is the place you're supposed to be is if the pastor's message bears witness, to what God is speaking to you. Keep in mind, it must line up with God's Word.

Eventually we did find a church to attend in Arizona, but I always knew Mount Zion would be our home church. Now remember, Karen's participation in church activities up until this time had been very sporadic. It was really strange to watch my wife enter into worship and praise. But what was more exciting than that was to see her continued growth in every area.

Before my wife's aneurysm, I used to talk to her about spiritual things, and she would look at me like she had no idea what I was talking about. She would sometimes even tell me so, but now it was like she had become a new person. I don't know where she went when she was in a coma, but I knew it had been a good place.

You see, I believe that because of her aneurysm, God had given her a new brain. The reason I say this is because of her constant desire to learn more about God. I can remember every morning my wife would wake up and say, "This is a new day." Then one day we were watching television. We were watching Day star, I think, and my cousin, Pastor Loren, came on with his television ministry, "Call from the Mountain," and his first words were, "This is a new day."

My wife was extremely excited, about this message because those words were the same words she kept saying in rehab, and something exploded inside of her. Soon after, Karen started looking for books to read. I had a great deal of books. These were books that I had acquired over time, and I had kept them because of their messages. I don't keep books around if I don't feel they have anything important to say.

The first book Karen had selected was *The Purpose Driven Life*. We really enjoyed reading this book together. This is a book you can read over and over again and receive a new revelation every time. After that, we started reading my Cousin Loren's books. The first one was called *About Father's House*. The second one was *Discovering Favor with God*. I had already read these several times. (And these are books that need to be read again and again as well.) But these books were all new to Karen, and she was very enthused about reading them.

Then we read everything else we could find. One of her favorite books was the Bible, and her understanding was as though she had been reading it all of her life. She would tell me things it had taken me some thirty years to understand. Now we so enjoy our study time together, our prayer time together, and our praise time together. It has become a major part of our lives.

For three years, God prepared Karen and me for the ministry. But it didn't happen overnight! We started using God's gifts almost immediately. As we used them, He gave us more, and as He gave us more, other people started to notice. Before long, it seemed as though everyone was asking us to pray for them, and God was continuing to pour Himself into us.

Soon Karen started asking me questions about baptism. Since her aneurysm, Karen has never been satisfied with a casual walk with God, and she continues to want everything she can get. But I'll get back to her baptism in another chapter.

During this time of preparation while God was preparing us for the ministry. It wasn't a time when we just sat around and studied and prayed. It was a time when we exercised our gifts so those gifts would grow stronger. During those times, we knew God was speaking to us. He said, "I want you to get rid of all your stuff. Not just your physical possessions or material possessions but more importantly those things that are within you that hinder the building of my kingdom."

Those physical things or material possessions were easy for me to get rid of but it did take Karen a little longer to hear God on this particular matter. Keep in mind, this is not for everyone, but we knew it was something we had to do for now. (Don't go giving all of your material possessions away.) It was those things inside of us that were more difficult. Although, that is an ongoing process, line upon line, precept upon precept here a little, there a little.

We started to travel. We bought an RV to increase our mobility. We have traveled to forty-eight states, taking God's love into all those places. After all, God did say we would be ministers to ministers, and how true this has been.

One time in particular, Karen and I were staying in a small town in northern Arizona. Knowing the following day was

Sunday, we were looking for a church to attend. We decided to go downtown and look around, and I saw a fudge shop. Karen says it was a craft shop, but all I saw was fudge. Now I don't know if that was a miracle or not, because I always seem to find fudge shops. But anyway, after entering the store and talking to the attendant for a short time, we asked her if there was a good church in town.

She replied, "That depends on what you're looking for."

As things started to run through my mind, Karen and I replied together almost immediately, "We want it all."

She said without hesitation, "I know just the church. Where are you staying?" I told her we were staying in the RV Park. She said, "That's perfect! The church is only two blocks away."

That was great because we were not pulling a tow car. So on Sunday morning, we got up and headed for the church. It wasn't a large church, but after worship and praise and the pastor started to speak, we soon realized they did in fact have it all, or at least what we were looking for. The pastor was speaking the same message that God had been speaking to us. Although I could tell the pastor was a bit uncomfortable with this new message.

After the service, this young pastor and his wife came directly to us. I think it was either to welcome us or because God sent them to us. It doesn't matter; either way, God is always in control. We introduced ourselves and explained what our ministry was, and then I told him I had a word from God for him. As God started to speak through me, the pastor started to cry. Then Karen and I prayed for him, and by the laying on of hands, we were able to stir up the gifts of the Holy Spirit and bring revival. We could actually see the rain starting to fall.

I don't want you to think we have this massive ministry; that wouldn't be true. But God provides the people and provides us with a word for them. Sometimes it's only one person, and sometimes it's a group of people. But Karen and I have decided that whatever God has appointed for us to do, we will do. Our message is one of faith, hope, obedience, forgiveness, and love, not necessarily in that order. I for myself, think love for humanity is the most important part or love for one another. That's because love causes us to have forgiveness, and without forgiveness, we can never love with God's love. I believe that the two go hand in hand. If we can make these applications to our lives, then we will have hope.

In **(Matthew 6:9-13),** Jesus gives us the Lord's Prayer. But then afterward, in verses 14 and 15 of the same chapter, He gives an explanation of this prayer. **He says, "If you forgive men their trespasses, your heavenly father will also forgive you. But if you do not forgive men their trespasses, neither will your father forgive your trespasses."** Try to keep in mind that this is not a recommendation; it is a commandment. This is God's trademark.

Karen and I have learned that without forgiveness, our relationship with one another will never grow. Furthermore, we have come to realize that our relationship with one another is a direct reflection of our relationship with God, especially, but not limited to, the marriage relationship. He says if we say we love Him and we don't love others, it's not the truth.

If someone says, I love God, and hates his brother, he is a liar; for he who does not love his brother whom he has seen, how can he love God whom he has not seen? And this commandment we have from him; that he who

loves God must love his brother also. (1 John 4:20-21)

Whoever hates his brother is a murderer, and you know that no murderer has eternal life abiding in him. (1 John 3:15,)

We must love one another! Now I do realize that there is a season for everything. But when that season lasts for too long, it's time to seek God for a new season. Karen and I have realized that as our love relationship with one another grows and our intimacy with one another continues to increase, so does our intimacy and love relationship increase with God. In addition to this we have come to realize that without forgiveness, we can never obtain all of what God has to offer.

Some of today's churches have worked tirelessly to educate counselors to teach the people. I believe education is extremely important for us to know how to treat one another, but we also need to realize that knowledge is not the most important key. **Second Timothy 3:7 says, "Always learning and never able to come to the knowledge of the truth."** This Scripture is talking about people who continue to learn but never come to know the truth. What truth? The truth about who Jesus Christ is, and what He came here to do.

You see, our hearts, or soil need to be prepared, and the only way for that to happen is to come into God's presence. If the soil of our hearts is not prepared, that seed will never grow. Some churches have forgotten this principle. That's the easy way. There is another way. I believe because of our reluctance to enter into His presence through worship and praise, God uses other things to prepare our hearts or soil, like tribulation Look at **(John 16:-33) "These things I have spoken to**

you, that in Me you may have peace. In the world you will have tribulation: but be of good cheer: I have overcome the world." (Galatians 3:3) says, "Are you so foolish? Having begun in the spirit, are you now being made perfect by the flesh?) We start out, in the spirit, and somehow get back into the flesh."

We think if we pack ourselves with enough knowledge through education that this is going to bring change. After all, knowledge let's say secular knowledge has so changed the world to this point. There is no more hatred, no more discrimination, no more hunger, no more wars, no more unwanted pregnancies, no more sexually transmitted diseases, and so on and so on. (I'm sure you get my point.)

We should know as Christians that it's the Spirit that brings change, along with God's Word. This doesn't mean we should neglect our education. What it does mean is that we should use our education in conjunction with the gifts of the Spirit. Karen and I have developed, through the Holy Spirit, certain techniques that God has taught us to use. One of those techniques is to enter into His presence prior to the planting of seed into their soil. Another is, the knowledge that we have received through education and forty-six years of marital experience, and application through the Holy Spirit. If two people are not willing to follow this procedure, anything God may have to say through us will not be received. Furthermore, as I mentioned earlier, without the preparation of our soil through entering into His presence, forgiveness for one another can't be obtained. Without forgiveness, things will never change.

Karen and I have learned to discern a person's spiritual location, as far as their presence before God, prior to the sowing of these seeds. The results of this process have been absolutely overwhelming. Remember, God is not out to restore marriages to their original state; He wants to restore marriages to what they were originally intended to be. If your marriage was what it was supposed to be, it would not be in the place that it is in (divorce). If we continue to take the same road, we will always wind up in the same destination.

God has shared His heart and this vision with us to show us what He is looking for in our marriages and our relationships with one another. He says if we will apply these visions and these principles to our marriages and relationships, His kingdom will come like a bolt of lightning, and His kingdom will be established in us, just as it will be established on earth. God says He will give us a vision of His Kingdom and how to establish that Kingdom.

Chapter 11

VISIONS

Okay, now were going to talk about visions. You're probably thinking, U*h oh, here we go again; not another vision.* The reason I say this is because I've heard a lot of visions, a lot of dreams, and so on and so forth, and many times I've thought to myself, W*ow, I think you better keep those to yourself.* But here goes.

Karen and I had traveled to Michigan for the annual family reunion. It's something Karen and I look forward to every year. We usually stay for six months or until it gets too cold. This is a time when Karen and I go home to see the family and also to receive a refreshing of the Holy Spirit. This is where our home church is, and this is where we go to receive our spiritual food when we are there. (Keep in mind, church isn't our only means of our spiritual food; we must also worship, praise, study God's Word, and seek God continuously.)

While we were there this time, we knew we wanted to put together a written testimony that we could share with others. So when we met with one of the counselors at church about this testimony, she mentioned that we should also share a message about marriage. I responded immediately by saying, "I don't think that's what God wants us to do. After all, what could I possibly have to say about marriage?"(I had almost forgotten that I knew everything) (Ha Ha)

I didn't think God had called Karen and I to do that type of ministry. We were told everything we needed to do to prepare our testimony. We headed home and started working on our testimony, but after a few days, those words were starting to haunt me. I decided to seek God about this thing. I said, "Lord, I don't know anything about marriage! If you want me to intervene in marriages, you're going to have to teach me."

I continued to seek God for several days with no answer. On one night in particular, I was up most of the night (*Holding Hands with God*). I finally fell asleep, and I woke up around seven o'clock. I got up to make coffee, which somehow has become my job. I don't know when it became my job, but I know it's my job. (Hey, come to think of it, I have acquired lots of those jobs.) I made coffee and went back to bed. As soon as I sat on the bed, God showed me a vision. Oh, and by the way I was glad it was a vision and not a dream. **(As Joel 2:28) says, "Your old men shall dream dreams" "Your young" men shall see visions."** I'm glad I still have visions.

This vision was of a vast amount of people. Couples, husbands and wives in this massive auditorium. Husbands were asking their wives for forgiveness, and that forgiveness was being given freely, and in turn, wives were asking forgiveness, and that forgiveness was being given freely, without hesitation. As this forgiveness was being given freely, scales started to fall from their eyes and their ears. Rain started to fall, and everyone in the auditorium was receiving this rain freely.

God said, "If you will go and teach these things that I teach you to my people, divorce among My people will someday be a thing of the past. As My people find intimacy with one another, their intimacy with Me will start to blossom."

As I lay back down in bed, God continued to show me the things that needed to be done, to make marriages what He originally intended for them to be. As I lay there in bed, there was no way I could go back to sleep, so I got up and waited patiently for Karen to wake up. Well, not exactly patiently; after all, I'm not the most patient person in the world.

When Karen woke up, with a little bit of help from me, I started to tell her about my vision. As I did, I started going through a step by step reconstruction of what God had told me about marriages and what needed to be done within the marriage relationship. As I did, Karen all of a sudden asked me, "Are you asking me for forgiveness?" I said, "Yes, I guess I am."

God spoke to me immediately and said, "This is not just for other people. This vision that I have shown you has to start here." Then I proceeded to get down on one knee, just as God had instructed me to do, and was instructing me to do now. I'm not going to go through the entire thing; it would take too long.

I started by asking my wife for forgiveness for everything. The reason I say everything is because I'm not sure I can remember in every way I have said things or done things to hurt her, or cause her to feel inferior. I could see and feel the closeness and intimacy we were sharing together, and immediately after I finished, Karen followed suit. She didn't get down on one knee, but she did hold my hand and look directly into my eyes. It was as though she knew exactly what to say even though I had never told her what God had said for her to say.

Then scales started falling from our eyes and our ears, and then rain started to drench both of us. I knew immediately that this vision was truly from God. I know all of us harbor feelings of un-forgiveness because we have become comfortable with it.

I'm not sure in what capacity God is going to use Karen and me to use these teachings. However, these things that God has taught us about marriage have become an intricate part of our relationship and has caused our marriage to grow. As our relationship with one another continues to grow, our relationship with God has grown miraculously. Now God has given Karen and me the opportunity to use this within the confines of the marriage relationship.

I will share one of those encounters with you. Karen and I had decided to go to South Dakota to a Christian concert. It's called Hills Alive, and I'm here to tell you they are alive. We try to attend this concert on a yearly basis. It's absolutely phenomenal. Just imagine, between forty thousand and fifty thousand Christians, all worshiping and praising God at the same time.

We decided this year we were going to take my sister Yolonda. We knew she had been having some difficult times and she needed to get away. Her job requires that she work almost every Sunday, and it makes it very difficult for her to grow spiritually. After the first day as night was starting to descend, a new group had taken the stage. They were sharing their testimony with us. When they were finished sharing their testimony, they asked that we break off into small groups to pray for one another.

Karen, Yolonda, and I selected a couple, or should I say God selected them, for us to minister to. The reason I say this is because they were looking directly at us. We asked them what their prayer request was. They told us their prayer request. We started to pray for them, but I knew in my heart that this was not the prayer request they needed. They asked us to pray for their finances. Not wanting to embarrass them, we finished our prayer for them and went back to worship and praise.

As we did, God started speaking to me about what the real problem was. He told me all about their marriage and what was going on within their marriage. Then He said, "I want you to use the things that I've taught you to bring this marriage back to life."

I said, "Father, are you sure that this is what you want me to say? I'm going to feel stupid if it isn't true."

He said, "Yes, I'm sure. Now is the time."

After worship and praise, I said to them, "God has a word for you. "They walked over to us immediately with open ears and hearts that were prepared by worship and praise. I asked, "How is your marriage?"

They looked at one another and then back at us, and both started to cry and went on to explain that their marriage was over! This would be the last time they would be together. God started speaking to me and telling me exactly what to say and not only what to say but what to do. I had them face one another hold hands, and I said, "Repeat after me."

As they did, I could see the miracle of God's restoration. Yes, the restoration of love and forgiveness flowed out from them like rivers of living water. It even flowed on to us and others who were standing around. I could see this flood because I had seen it before in a vision. Now keep in mind that this was taking place in front of thousands of people. Karen says that it was almost as though they were renewing their wedding vows. With the way they embraced when this ceremony was complete, Karen said, "I think they're going to be just fine." This is what I believe the Bible refers to as God's Glory presence.

You see, this was part of the vision God had shown me about how the church needs to adopt this principle prior to the planting of the seed into their soil or heart. In this vision that God gave us, He said, "My people need to come into My presence through worship and praise, so I can prepare their hearts, because without that preparation of their hearts, or soil, any seed that might be planted will not grow."

See the parable of the sower. Read (Matthew13:3–8) and then the explanation of that parable in the same chapter (19–23). Then in (Jeremiah 4:3) God is speaking to all of us when He says, **"Break up your fallow ground, and do not sow among the thorns."** Fallow ground by definition, is soil that has become unproductive or hard, because of non use.

This is just one of the marriages God has used Karen and me to restore to what God requires a marriage to be, to establish His kingdom. Sometimes we Christians want to apply knowledge that we have received through education, but we soon forget to apply the Holy Spirit along with what we have learned. We do realize that education is extremely important, but we also realize education by itself will never bring us to the destination that God wants us at. God starts us out in the spirit, and somehow we wind up back in the flesh.

But try to remember, this is a new day! God will no longer allow us to stay in the flesh. **(Galatians 3:3) says, "Are you so foolish? Having begun in the spirit, are you now being made perfect by the flesh?"** When we Christians realize that we are no longer in bondage to the old covenant law of marriage, our marriages will start to blossom. I know this sounds really scary to a lot of us, but until we can let go of the old and embrace the new, our marriages will never be what God intended for them to be. But if we embrace this new covenant, it will give us the freedom to nurture the love relationship God always intended for us to have. Remember, if the old l covenant would have been adequate, we wouldn't have needed a new covenant

For if that first covenant had been faultless, then no place would have been sought for a second. Because finding fault with them, He says: "Behold, the days are coming, says the Lord, when I will make a new covenant with the house of Israel and with the house of Judah "not according to the covenant that I made with their fathers in the day when I took them by the hand to lead them out of the land of Egypt; because they did not continue in My covenant, and I disregarded them, says the Lord. "For this is the covenant that I will make with the house of Israel after those days, says the Lord: I will put My laws in their mind and write them on their hearts; and I will be their God, and they shall be My people. In that He says, "A new covenant," He has made the first obsolete. Now what is becoming obsolete and growing old is ready to vanish away. (Hebrews 8: 7-10, 13)

Don't you see that He takes away the first so He may establish the second, the second what? The second covenant. Keep in mind that the old covenant stands in the way of the new covenant, which is that of love and forgiveness. **(John13:34 says, "A new commandment I give to you, that you love one another; as I have loved you, that you also love one another."** If you have forgiveness and love for your spouse, the old covenant laws of marriage won't be needed.

(First Corinthians 13:10) says, "But when that which is perfect has come, then that which is in part will be done away." God's talking about something that is perfect here. He's talking about love, and then He talks about that which is in part, which is the law. Remember, God tells us that the law was given to us as a tutor until that which is perfect has come, which is love.

(Galatians 3:24,) "Therefore, the law was our tutor to bring us to Christ, that we might be justified by faith." Faith in what? Faith in Jesus Christ. We know that Jesus is love. We need to know that the marriage covenant is a reflection of God's love covenant with us. That original contract or covenant is used as a tutor until that which is perfect has come, which is love!

Okay next vision! This next vision is about heaven and hell. One day as I was looking around the church I was attending in Arizona, I noticed how much the women outnumbered the men. As I continued to notice this, I realized this wasn't just a problem in Arizona. Keep in mind that Karen and I have been in all forty eight lower states. This was the situation in every church we attended, so I started to seek God about this matter (*Holding Hands with God*).

I sought God most of the night for an answer but finally fell asleep. When I awoke in the morning and sat up in the bed, God showed me another vision. There was this man, and he was in hell. This place was the most horrible place you could possibly imagine. I won't go into any detail, but I will say one of the worst things about this place was the absence of God's presence.

Then all of a sudden this man's son walked in and said, "Hello, Dad."

His dad said, "Son, what are you doing here! Didn't I tell you how to live your life and tell you which direction you should go?" "Didn't I send you to church?"

He said, "Yes, Dad, but I loved you so much I wanted to be just like you, so I followed your lead."

And then that boy's son walked in, and this happened over and over and over again until this place was full. Then God showed me heaven, and there was this man. In this beautiful, magnificent place, he was worshiping and praising God, and then his son walked in.

He said, "Son! I'm so happy to see you."

The son said, "Father, I am so happy to be here. I am so glad that you walked in the direction that you walked and that you revealed Christ's Kingdom to me, so that I walked in the same direction."

I can remember back when I was around thirty four years old, shortly after my visitation from God. I looked at my three sons and prayed, "Lord, I don't like some of the things I see in my sons."

God spoke to me again, He said, "If you don't like what you see in your sons, it's because those very same things are in you. If you want change in them, you need to change first." As God continued to speak, He went on to say, "I promise you this very day, if you will make these changes that I reveal to you in yourself by seeking me, I will make these changes in your children."

I said, "Father, I will do everything You ask me to do, regardless of the pain it causes me, and make whatever changes are needed, because the buck stops here."

Now I look at my sons and see the fruits of these changes. I can see Christ in them and in their children. (My beautiful Grandchildren) Keep in mind, this didn't happen overnight. **(Isaiah 28:-10) says, "For precept must be upon precept, precept upon precept, line upon line, line upon line, here a little and there a little."**

This vision isn't just for men; it encompasses the women as well as brothers, sisters, aunts, uncles, cousins, and friends all of us. This is something we need to know. If we don't take the responsibility to teach our children by example and lead them in the right direction, they're going to follow someone else. Remember our ungodly words, actions, and activities are like a poison. We feed it to our children, and when they grow up, we wonder why their sick.

Now is the time when we need to stand up as kings and priests in our household, and I am not talking about a dictatorship either, if you know what I mean. Although many times, I have felt like a dictator raising three boys. (Ha ha)

Now Karen and I have realized that as we come together in unity, our children become a product of that unity. As we walk after Christ, our children walk in that same direction. That's one of the many reasons Karen and I think unity in the family is just as important as it is in the church or even more so. You can't have one, without the other.

Chapter 12

UNITY IN THE BODY OF CHRIST

When God first spoke to me about unity early on, it was about unity within my marriage and how difficult it would be. What I didn't realize was how difficult this task would be in the rest of the body of Christ. You talk about unity to other Christians, and they'll tell you, "Yes, we need unity," but what they're really saying is we need for all the other people to believe the exact same way as we do, because we know we have it right.

I'm not saying that we should adopt a bunch of cockamamie beliefs in order to have unity; this is not what I'm talking about. I do realize that there are a number of beliefs that have no apparent connection to God's Word, at least not the way I see it. I'm talking about smaller issues like if once saved you are always saved, whether you can lose your salvation, or what exactly you believe about the rapture. Now that's a topic that's all over the place, and I don't understand why. After all, do any of our beliefs change what's going to happen? Or does it say somewhere in God's Word that you have to understand the rapture to be saved? Not anywhere that I have read.

Some people believe that there is going to be this great falling away and that many of God's people are going to somehow be plucked out of His hand and start serving the antichrist. I don't believe this for a second. Both (Deuteronomy

31:8) and (Hebrews 13:5) tell us that God will never leave us or forsake us.

Some people have actually made the rapture theory into a religion, and that's all they want to talk about. Some people even say we need to pray that the Lord comes soon before the enemy converts all of God's people to himself. I want you to know that this is not God's plan. Furthermore, God has no intention of surrendering any of His children to the enemy.

I can remember very early in my walk with Christ, after talking with lots of Christians, I adopted a very similar viewpoint, but one night as I was praying (*Holding hands with God*) God spoke to me very plainly. He said, "My people need to quit worrying about the rapture and start thinking about the capture."

After all, when you think about it, how many people do you know who haven't accepted Christ? Again I ask how does what we think about the rapture affect our salvation? I think if anything we should be praying that He should hold off for a time.

The other day as I was going for my walk, I saw a bumper sticker. It said, "Jesus is coming soon, and is He pissed." I would think it should say, "Jesus is coming soon, and is He pleased?" I could go on and on, but I'm sure you get my point. I don't think some of these things can ever be totally agreed upon. And besides, all of those things that bring division in the body of Christ should not even be an issue.

(Mark 9:38–41 says,)

John was talking to Jesus, and he said Teacher. We saw some people down the road,

**casting out demons in your name, and we told
them not to do it anymore, because they were
not a member of our club, or denomination,
and Jesus said to them. Do not forbid them to
do works and miracles in my name. For if they
are not against us they are on our side. No one
can give a cup of water to drink in my name,
and not be one of mine.**

As I said earlier in this book, we need to realize that all of
God's children are in a different place spiritually. If we think we
are more mature, we should have the patience to nurture and
bring others to a new spiritual location, just as God, through
His patience and love, brings us to this new spiritual location.
Let's take another look at **(John 14:2-3) Jesus says:**

**In my father's house are many mansions;
if it were not so, I would have told you. I go
to prepare a place for you. "And if I go and
prepare a place for you, I will come again and
receive you to myself; that where I am, there
you may be also.**

Jesus is talking about a place of maturity He has ascended
to, not a large castle in the sky, or at least this is what I believe
it says in the New King James Version. Some of the other
translations say, "In my Father's house there are many rooms,"
or "In my Father's house there are many houses," but I like the
New King James Version. That's what I read, and that's what I
study. It's not that the other translations are incorrect; it's just
that I like this one the best.

Now you know that our place in heaven has already been
secured, if we have been born again. What we need to realize

is that God is talking about our growth or spiritual maturity right here and right now. He goes on to say in **(John14: 6) "I am the way the truth and the life. No one comes to the Father except through me."** To me this scripture, along with **(Mark 9:38-41)** is again referencing unity and spiritual maturity. As our personal relationship with Christ continues to grow, our unity, spiritual maturity, and love for humanity will continue to grow as well. We should also realize that the most important commandment God wants us to know is that we must love the Lord with all we have within us. And we must love one another. By keeping these two commandments, we will fulfill every commandment.

In **(John 13:34-35) Jesus says, "A new commandment I give to you, that you love one another; as I have loved you, that you also love one another. By this everyone will know that you are my disciples, if you have love for one another."** God is not making a suggestion that we should love one another. After all, this is a commandment and supersedes all other commandments. And again in **(Luke 10: 27,) it says. "You shall love the Lord your God with all your heart, with all your soul, with all your strength, and with all your mind,' and your neighbor as yourself."**

Furthermore, we need to realize that, in order to love one another, there must be forgiveness. This love can only come from God; it's not something we can muster up on our own. I'm not talking about when you're driving down the street and someone runs you off the road and starts making obscene gestures that you should run to them and hug and kiss them. Although, I've never tried that it might work. My first thought isn't how much I love that individual. It's that I would like to lay hands on that person, and I actually have, on a few occasions. Now that I've gotten older, I hope that I've matured beyond that point. Besides, I'm getting too old for that type of behavior, and I don't want to get hurt.

What I'm talking about is the forgiveness we need to have for one another so love can abound. See (Philippians 1:9) this is the love and unity that I'm talking about. Because we know that God says love is the answer. We need to all realize that we come from different ethnic backgrounds. We were all raised differently, and sometimes some of our beliefs are going to be different. I'm not saying that we should put aside sound doctrine; I'm just saying we need to make sure it's something we want to go to war about, knowing that God leads all of His people to the truth in His time. We have to always remember, that God never starts a work that He doesn't finish.

Okay, that's enough said about unity, even though I have a great deal more to say. I'm not going to say it in this book. Since this is my last chapter, I would like to get back to the miracle of my wife, Karen. As I mentioned earlier in this book, Karen had mentioned baptism to me. As we discussed her baptism in detail she said, "I would love to get baptized at Mount Zion." She went on to explain why. She said, "My whole family" (In reference to Jim, Marc, Tim, and I had all been baptized at Mount Zion.) She went on to say, "I love what I see in all of you, and would love to experience the same thing."

This was exciting to me, and when we arrived in Michigan, I started making arrangements for her baptism. The day Pastor Loren chose was a Tuesday morning prayer service. Prior to her baptism, her spiritual growth was phenomenal; after her baptism, it was supernatural. What was more amazing is that on the day of her baptism, there were several hundred people there. We didn't plan it that way; it just happened. There were a lot of people there who had given me a prophetic word about my wife some thirty years earlier. They reminded me of those words that were spoken over my wife.

Then I started remembering some of the things the hospital staff had spoken to me, such as, "Your wife will never be able to make decisions on her own." I thought to myself, *that's true, my wife doesn't make decisions on her own; God plays a big part in her decision making.* They said, "She will never be the same person." This is true; she is not the same person. She is becoming the woman God intended for her to be. Now she is a godly person. They said, "Your wife will never be able to walk on her own." This is true. She doesn't walk on her own; she walks after God now. They said, "Your wife will never have her own thoughts again." This is mostly true; her thoughts are usually not her own. I'm not going to elaborate on this. It might get me in trouble (just joking). They said, "Your wife will be totally dependent," This is true as well; she is totally dependent on God.

I thought to myself, *Wow! All that time in the hospital, God was speaking to me through the hospital staff, and I didn't receive Him.* **(John 1: 11,) He came to His own, and His own did not receive Him.** Then I started thinking about how Karen and I have come together as one. I don't want you to think that we don't have differences of opinion, but the love we share now supersedes any of our differences or disagreements. You see, our old marriage covenant has passed away, and our new covenant of love and forgiveness is now functioning as it was originally intended.

As Karen and I walk together to build God's kingdom and as we grow closer and closer, we realize now that God did have a plan for us all these years, but we couldn't see it because of the scales on our eyes. Now Karen and I together see that we along with you, God's people, and this means you are, His plan. We have been His plan since time began, from the very beginning, and we will continue to be His plan until the end, or should I say the beginning. **(John 1:4) says, "In Him was life, and the life was the light of**

men." All of us need to come to the realization of who we are in Christ and who He is in us. Both Karen and I together have learned to *Hold Hands with God. This is not the end; This is the Beginning.*